Prayer – The Heart of it All
Biblical Principles with Practical Models

P. Douglas Small

Prayer – The Heart of It All
Biblical Principles and Practical Models

ISBN: 978-0-9896525-5-1

©Copyright 2017 by P. Douglas Small

Published by Alive Publications
a division of
Alive Ministries: PROJECT PRAY
PO Box 1245

Kannapolis, NC 28082

www.alivepublications.org
www.projectpray.org

All rights reserved. No part of this publication may be reproduced, stored in a retrieval system, or transmitted in any form by any means (printed, written, photocopied, visual electronic, audio, digital or otherwise) without the prior permission from the publisher. The exception being brief quotations with appropriate reference documentation and the use of the material for teaching and training.

Consider *Prayer – The Heart of It All Study Guide,* a companion Personal and Group Study Guide. *Prayer – The Heart of It All* Resource Kit is even more complete with Teaching Guide, PowerPoint and videos tied to the book and teaching guide. Available at www.alivepublications.org.

Dedication

The first version of this book I dedicated to the pastors of my home church in my growing up years – the late S. A. Lankford, Walter Barwick, C. L. Leonard, and Henry J. Smith – powerful mentors. And, to the sound of the intercessors of that church, whose voices offered in passionate prayer still ring in my heart.

This extensive revision, I dedicate to my grandchildren in hopes that the devotional times Barbara, my wife, and I have spent with them will never be forgotten.

To Nicholas (and Lexa), Ian, Reagan and Daci Wilbanks;
Hannah, Jack, Liberty and Joseph Hollifield;
Kassidy, Mackenzie, Katie and Coleton Burke;
Emma, Harper, Caden and Chandler Small
Layla and Ellie Greene

Foreword

By Phil Miglioratti

*Epaphras, who is one of you and a servant
of Christ Jesus sends greetings.
He is always wrestling for you in prayer, so that, you stand firm
in all the will of God, mature and fully assured.
I vouch for him that he is working hard for you
and for those at Laodicea and Heiropolos.*

Years ago the Lord used this scripture to open my eyes and heart to a deeper-and-wider understanding of prayer. Since then, Epaphras has been my prayer mentor. Doug Small reminds me of Epaphras.

Epaphras though his name hints that his parents may have dedicated him to Aphrodite, the goddess of love, he seems to have become a beloved man of prayer. Doug writes from that same devotion to love. From this 21st century Epaphras, you will learn first and foremost to pray from and with love. Scan the Table of Contents. You'll discover prayer as love; God loving us through prayer and our love of communion with God. Love-for-family prompts praying. Love moves us to pray with the Church. The extension of God's love is demonstrated through praying for lost persons and nations. Doug writes from a love-motivated heart and demonstrates how that kind of praying must be at the heart of everything.

Like Epaphras, Doug is *"one of us."* An ordinary guy who serves with extraordinary energy in using the gifts the Spirit has bestowed upon him. His knowledge is comprehensive and his insights strategic. When you read, please slow down to ponder before rushing on to the next section or chapter. Your goal is not to ingest the book as quickly as possible but to digest the wonderful confluence of scripture, explanation and application. But (and Doug would certainly agree), do not be fooled by his deep-and-wide wisdom; his challenges and admonitions are not limited to the super-stars of prayer. Like the great prophet Elijah, he is just like us (James 5:17).

Like Epaphras, Doug understands praying as an expression of being *a servant of Christ Jesus*. And his teachings reveal praying in the name of Jesus is an act of service, not the delivery of a "What I want for Christmas" shopping list. Servant is our identify and service is our assignment. Prayer is how we express our identity and how we receive those assignments.

The apostle said, Epaphras *"sends greetings."* He must have cared about the people he stood with in his intercession. The teachings in this book come from the heart of a man of God who cares about the people who are reading, thinking about, and implementing prayer insights. Prayer is relational; with God and with people.

The Apostle describes Epaphras a one who *wrestled in prayer* for the people he loved. The term for wrestle transliterates to "agonize." As I look back again to the Table of Contents, I envision an author who has wrestled with foundational and advanced issues for both beginners and prayer veterans.

"So that." Epaphras has taught me that these two words are essential in the simplest and briefest of prayers. Petitions to help, bring hope, for healing, must not stop with the request. Beginning with the problem, trouble, or need, every prayer must push through to God's purpose or promise. *"So that."* So that every prayed for person grows beyond their need to become a Christ-follower who *"stands firm." "In all the will of God."* More *"mature"* as a result of the situation. *"Fully assured,"* confident the next time they face a trail. *Prayer – The Heart of it All* is a resource for disciplemaking.

The Apostle said he could *"vouch for (Epaphras) that he is working hard for you."* Doug has done that for us in this book. So that one day someone will be able to say the same about our faithfulness in prayer.

The Apostle adds that Epaphras works hard in *prayer for those in two other cities.* This is no trivial comment. Doug understands that our praying must go beyond our personal needs, beyond family and friends, beyond our congregation. He introduces us to missional praying. Prayer evangelism. Nation-changing praying. The need for the Church to pray for the advancement of the Gospel against the radical and rapid shifts in culture is crucial and urgent. Prayer – must be at the heart of it ALL.

ASV – Scripture quotations marked "ASV" are taken from the American Standard Version Bible (Public Domain).

BBE – The Bible in Basic English Bible (BBE) is in the public domain.

ESV – Scripture quotations marked "ESV" are from the ESV Bible® (The Holy Bible, English Standard Version®), copyright © 2001 by Crossway Bibles, a publishing ministry of Good News Publishers. Used by permission. All rights reserved.

GWT – GOD'S WORD is a copyrighted work of God's Word to the Nations. Scripture Quotations marked "God's Word" are used by permission. Copyright, 1995, by God's Word to the Nations. Used by permission of Baker Publishing Group. All rights reserved.

NASB – Scripture quotations marked "NASB" are taken from the New American Standard Bible®, Copyright © 1960, 1962, 1963, 1968, 1971, 1972, 1973, 1975, 1977, 1995 by The Lockman Foundation. Used by permission.

NKJV – All scripture quotations, unless otherwise indicated, are taken from the New King James Version®. Copyright © 1982 by Thomas Nelson, Inc. Used by permission. All rights reserved.

KJV – King James Version. Scripture quotations marked "KJV" are taken from the Holy Bible, King James Version, Cambridge, 1769.

NIV – New International Version. Scripture quotations marked "NIV" are taken from HOLY BIBLE, NEW INTERNATIONAL VERSION. Copyright: 1973, 1978, 1984 by International Bible Society. Used by permission of Zondervan Publishing House.

NLT – New Living Translation. Scripture quotations marked "NLT" are taken from the Holy Bible, New Living Translation, copyright 1996. Used by permission of Tyndale House Publishers, Inc., Wheaton, Illinois 60189. All rights reserved.

TLB – The Living Bible. Scripture quotations marked "TLB" or "The Living Bible" are taken from The Living Bible [computer file] / Kenneth N. Taylor. electronic ed. Wheaton : Tyndale House, 1997, c1971 by Tyndale House Publishers, Inc. Used by permission. All rights reserved.

WBT – Webster Bible Translation. Containing the Old and New Testaments, in the Common Version, with Amendments of the Language, by Noah Webster, LL D. Public. • ALL RIGHTS RESERVED • First printing, November, 2011

Contents

Seven Commitments of a Praying Church 15
Ten Prayer Values 16

Section One - Growing in Prayer

CHAPTER 1: What is Prayer? 23
- Three Aspects of Prayer 26
  - ◊ Communion with God
    - » More than Meditation
    - » It Demands Speech
    - » It is Praying Beyond Words
    - » It is Unity with the Spirit
- Why God Wants Us to Pray 30
  - ◊ God Loves Company
  - ◊ Prayer is a Privilege
  - ◊ Prayer is Heaven's Way of Blessing
  - ◊ Prayer Taps the Bounty in the Endowment of Christ
  - ◊ Prayer's Basis of Appeal – Covenant Promises
  - ◊ Prayer Invites the Kingdom of God

CHAPTER 2: What Prayer Says About God 39
- Back to the Beginning 39
  - ◊ God Wants to Talk to You
  - ◊ What God is Saying
  - ◊ Prayer and Blessing
  - ◊ Heightening Spiritual Sensitivity
    - » Inset: The Fall of Man and the Serpent
- Seeing Prayer's Bigger Picture 47
  - ◊ The Natural or the Spiritual
  - ◊ Triggering Discernment
  - ◊ Coming Out of Hiding
- God – the Seeker 50
  - ◊ Prayer and the God Who Gives
  - ◊ Prayer and the God Who Gives Grace
  - ◊ Prayer and the God Who Redeems and Disciplines
  - ◊ Prayer – the Place of Promise and Hope
- Our Pursuing God 53

CHAPTER 3: What Prayer Says About Us..........55
- God is Waiting
- We Should Be Seeking
- What Not Seeking Says About Us..........56
- Truth Avoidance and Prayerlessness..........57
- Pursuing God
  ◊ Seeking Him
    » God – the Real Goal of Prayer
    » Believing – Where We Put Our Faith
    » Doubting God's Character – is Deadly
  ◊ Joining Prayer and Love
    » Faith Works by Love
    » Praying in Love's Embrace
  ◊ Switching Motives for Prayer
    » Praying for Answers
    » Meeting Conditions
    » Praying Amiss
      » Inset: Honesty and Grace
    » Inverting Motives in Prayer
  ◊ Moving from Answers to Rewards

SECTION TWO - PERSONAL AND FAMILY PRAYER

CHAPTER 4: Personal Prayer – The Defining Mark of a Christian ... 71
  » Inset: Indicators of a Personal Relationship with Christ
- Marks of An Effective Prayer Life..........74
  ◊ Prayer and the Secret Place
  ◊ Prayer – The Secret to Spiritual Power
    » Inset: Suggested Items in a Personal Prayer Room
  ◊ Prayer – Moving from Duty to Delight
    » Inset: Prayer Treasure Hunt
  ◊ Prayer – Worshipful Love
  ◊ Prayer – The Empowerment to Action
  ◊ Prayer – As a Means of Filtering Toxic Thoughts
  ◊ Prayer Over an Open Bible
  ◊ Prayer as a Means of Purification
  ◊ Living in an Atmosphere of Prayer
  ◊ Prayer as Transformational
    » Inset: Ten Ways to Deepen Your Communion with God

Contents

CHAPTER 5: The Process of Personal Prayer 91
- ◊ Pray Always
- ◊ Pray According to the Word
- ◊ Prayer with the Enabling of the Holy Spirit
- ◊ Pray in the Name of Jesus
- ◊ Pray that God be Glorified
- ◊ Pray to the Judge of the Universe, the Father
- ◊ Pray Submitting to the Will of God
- ◊ Pray with Eternal Kingdom Purposes in View
- Summary 98
- Conclusion
  - » Inset: Involving Your Body in Prayer

CHAPTER 6: Family and Faith 101
- Faith in the Home 102
  - » Inset: Bless Your Children
- Couples Praying Together 105
  - ◊ The Christian Difference
  - ◊ The Prayer Difference
  - ◊ Prayer Implications for a Couple
  - ◊ Prayer Goals for a Couple
  - » Inset: Couple's Prayer
- Church at Home 110
- Let the Children Pray 112

CHAPTER 7: The Family Altar 115
- » Inset: Praying with and for Your Kids
- ◊ Changing Times
  - » Inset: Family Altar Dedication
- ◊ Renewing the Practice of the Family Altar
- ◊ A Physical Space
  - » Inset: House Dedication
- Our Jewish Prayer Heritage 122
  - ◊ The Family in Prayer
  - ◊ The Feast Days – Faith Celebrations
    - » Inset: Keep a Family Journal
  - ◊ A Family Faith Calendar
    - » Inset: Prayer Treks
- Conclusion 126

Section Three - The Church and Prayer

CHAPTER 8: Praying in the Two Big Blessing Circles..................131
- Prayer – Home and Church 131
  ◊ At-Home Daily Prayer
  ◊ The Church at Prayer
    » Inset: Ways to Measure the Seriousness of the Churches
  ◊ The Church's Prayer Ministry
    » Commitment to Prayer
  ◊ Praying Corporately
    » Inset: Circles of Prayer
  ◊ Praying with Variety
    » Inset: Nursery Prayer
    » Inset: Suggestions for Prayer and Petition
    » Inset: Creating a Circle of Prayer for the Pastor

CHAPTER 9: The Church – A House of Prayer..............................149
- The Church and Power 149
  ◊ Prayer and the Miraculous
  ◊ Prayer and Power
    » Inset: Revival of Prayer
  ◊ Prayer and Witness
  ◊ Prayer and Character
    » Inset: Getting Started with a Prayer Ministry
  ◊ Prayer and Unity
- Three Kinds of Churches 161
    » Inset: Preaching and Prayer – and Preaching and Prayer

CHAPTER 10: Missional Praying 167
- Identify Intercessors 167
  ◊ Identify
  ◊ Train
  ◊ Team
    » Inset: Intercessors on Alert
  ◊ Direct
  ◊ Debrief
    » Inset: PIT Teams
- Prayer Evangelism 173
  ◊ Prayer and Passion
  ◊ This Age and Passion
    » Inset: Pray before You Play

Contents

◊ Prayer Evangelism Ideas

CHAPTER 11: The Strategic Position of Intercession 181
- Intercession: The Uncomfortable Middle 182
  ◊ Inset: From the Diary of David Brainerd
- Intercession: The Need for Persistence 184
- Intercession: The Problem of Interference 185
- Intercession: The Position of a Watchman 186
  ◊ Inset: Watchmen on the Wall
- Children as Intercessors 188
  ◊ Inset: Fifteen Subjective Identifiers of Intercessors
- Intercession and Spiritual Power 191

CHAPTER 12: Prayer Evangelism – The Extension of God's Love 195
- Prayer Evangelism 196
  ◊ The Gift of Prayer
    » Inset: Prayer Ambassadors
    » Inset: For Whom Should We Intercede?
  ◊ The Three Greats of the New Testament
- Intercession and the Lost 200
    » Inset: Prayers to Fulfill the Great Commission
    » Inset: Praying for Non-Believers
  ◊ Intercession: God Loving Through Us in Prayer
    » Inset: Kneeling in Prayer
  ◊ Intercession and the Character of God
  ◊ Intercession and the Heart of God
    » Inset: Prayer Precepts Taught by Jesus

SECTION FOUR - BACK TO THE FUTURE

CHAPTER 13: Nation-Changing Prayer 217
- Our National Spiritual History 217
    » Inset: A Man of Prayer in a Pagan Government
  ◊ The First Great Awakening
  ◊ Our National Beginnings
  ◊ The Second Great Awakening
    » Inset: Prayers for Cities and Nations
  ◊ The Third Great Awakening
  ◊ Azusa Street
  ◊ Camp Creek
- Needed! Another Great Awakening 229

- CHAPTER 14: Looking for a Vessel..233
  - Such a Pleasant Place...233
    - ◊ Bad Water
      - » Inset: Prayer Walking
    - ◊ Breaking the Spell
  - The Reality of Our Situation..237
    - ◊ Cultural Hostility toward Faith
    - ◊ Dirty Vessels Without Salt
  - Echoes from the Past and Distant Sounds 241
    - ◊ Cycles of Revival
    - ◊ Sounds of Awakening
    - ◊ Almolonga
    - ◊ Cali, Colombia
      - » Inset: How to Pray for Your Government Officials
    - ◊ Kiambu, Kenya
  - Could It Happen Again? 247
    - ◊ Needed – A Fresh Vessel
    - ◊ The Evan Roberts Formula

A Final Note.. 253

Seven Commitments of a Praying Church

1. Led by a praying pastor, and aided by a **PRAYER LEADERSHIP TEAM**, we commit to bring prayer to the heart of all we do! "Without Christ, we can do nothing!" Therefore, our resources, spiritual and material; our plans and programs, we will bathe in prayer.
2. We will encourage **AT-HOME, DAILY, TO-BE-LIKE-JESUS PRAYING**. We will reestablish our personal and family altars. We will embrace the discipline of daily times with God, with one another as couples, and as families. We will champion the idea of prayer rooms/closets.
3. We will call our congregation to persistent prayer with the goal of establishing **A REGULAR PRAYER MEETING** for the entire church at least monthly, if not, weekly. We will make the prayer meeting as important as Sunday Morning singing and preaching.
4. We will honor those who carry a special calling to pray – intercessors. **WE WILL IDENTIFY INTERCESSORS**, encourage them, train them, team them, deploy them and debrief them.
5. We will engage in **PRAYER EVANGELISM**, turning prayer outward onto the neighborhood, the city, state and nation – and we will adopt a mission field for prayer, one near and one far. We will pray for the harvest. We will seek to identify the people for whom God has made us most responsible, and we will begin the process of evangelism in prayer, look for ways to care, and steward the opportunities to share the gospel.
6. We will work toward the creation of a **PRAYER ROOM OR CENTER**, a physical space dedicated to prayer at our church, and we will encourage the use of such a space by members and prayer groups. We will provide resources for prayer – that run through all our departments, until we have a praying church, and not merely a prayer ministry.
7. We will offer regular **TRAINING** in the area of prayer – for our people, leaders, intercessors, prayer evangelism, our youth and children, our families.

Ten Prayer Values

1. We value prayer; therefore we will feature prayer in our worship and make prayer a central element of all ministry.
2. We are a praying people; therefore we will nurture at-home daily prayer, family prayer, husband-wife, parent-child prayer connections, providing resources, training and nudging new and old Christians to deepen their prayer lives.
3. We believe that we are a kingdom of priest and that prayer and worship is our highest calling, and that as priests we are not only recipients of blessing, but the conveyors of blessing; therefore, in prayer we choose to pray for the favor and blessing of God, protective care, upon our pastor, the church staff, the church family, our city and our nation. We bless, we do not curse. We ask God not for what we deserve, but for blessing – for continued grace and mercy!
4. We value holiness and righteousness, as the mark of God upon a people, and we recognize that the church desperately needs revival and our nation needs a great awakening; therefore we regularly and consistently cry out to God for revival in the church and a great awakening for our nation.
5. We believe in the power of petition, that God answers prayer; therefore we faithfully take the needs of the church, one another, the city and the world before the throne of God and ask for grace!

We provide a means whereby requests for prayer are taken seriously and held up in prayer persistently, beseeching God expectantly for an answer.

6. We believe in the power of intercession; therefore we identify, train, team and mobilize intercessors for the under-girding of the ministries of the Church, and for the support of the various mission endeavors of the congregation.

7. We believe that prayer is essential to the success of every endeavor, that without him we can do nothing, and whatever we do in his behalf without dependence upon Him is less than it might have been, given dependence in prayer; therefore, our rule is no one works, unless someone prays!

8. We believe that the reception of the gospel unto salvation is a spiritual issue; therefore, we pray for the harvest, that blind eyes will be open to the gospel; ears enabled to hear and receive the truth of Christ; hearts may receptive to the good news that goes forth in power, out of prayer.

9. We believe that there is definitive connection between prayer and the harvest; therefore, we insist that prayer must have a missional dimension, that we must pray for lost loved ones, for the unreached in our city and the world.

10. We believe, "God governs the world by the prayers of His people"; therefore, we pray for our city, state and national leaders. We pray about world conditions and various global crises.

Dan Rather was the anchor for CBS news for many years. In that role, he interviewed some of the most powerful and intimidating people on the face of the earth. But it was his interview with Mother Teresa that left him speechless.

Rather asked her, "When you pray, what do you say to God?" The question was reasonable. It assumed content, that the nexus of prayer was in its words.

"I don't say anything," the champion of the poor replied, "I listen."

Rather regrouped. "Well, okay...when God speaks to you, then, what does He say?"

That's when things got interesting. "He doesn't say anything. He listens," she responded.

Rather was bewildered. For a moment, he was completely baffled as to how to proceed. The little woman from Calcutta sat sweetly and quietly, and didn't seem inclined to make his task easier.

"And if you don't understand that," she added, "I can't explain it to you."[1]

George Buttrick says,

Prayer is listening as well as speaking...and its deepest mood is friendship held in reverence. So daily prayer should end as it begins – in adoration."[2]

Prayer is more than words!

SECTION ONE
Growing in Prayer

CHAPTER 1
What is Prayer?

There is a story told of a king who commissioned a contest among artists. Whoever could depict perfect peace on a canvas would win the King's admiration and a great treasure. Two entries remained as finalists for review. One setting was so serene it seemed the epitome of peace and tranquility. Oohs and ahs resounded from spectators as the painting was unveiled. Everything was well ordered. Nothing was out of place. It was a picture of perfect peace. It was, all assumed, the sure contest winner.

The second entry was then unveiled. It drew an immediate gasp. The canvas depicted anything but serenity. A massive waterfall dominated the scene. Angry white foam and spray could almost be felt near the painting, it seemed so real. The deafening roar of the rumbling falls was implicit. The sky was dark, laden with streaks of lightning. The painting shouted. A stormy sky. Thunder. Lightning. Rain. Tumbling and roaring water. It seemed the very opposite of peace.

Then someone noticed that in the center of the painting, behind the waterfall, in the cleft of the rock, a songbird had built a nest. Sheltered by the recessed rock, the songbird sat on her nest confidently joining nature's symphony as if she had been assigned a melodious solo. You could almost hear her sing. Everyone knew this was perfect peace. To be in the cleft of the rock in the middle of the raging storm – *and sing!*

"*In the world you will have tribulation,*" Jesus said, "*but in Me you will have peace*" (John 16:33). Peace is the effect on a heart that has been quieted by the unmistakable sense of God's presence. It is unbroken communion with Him – and that's the essence of prayer. Much of our current anxiety is traceable to the lack of a daily, consistent, unhurried time with God. When even our devotional times are frantic, expect little peace in other areas of life.

> What is the reason that some believers are so much brighter and holier than others? I believe the difference in nineteen cases out of twenty, arises from different habits about private prayer. I believe that those who are not eminently holy pray little and those who are eminently holy pray much.
>
> – J. C. Ryle

John Bunyan declared:

Prayer is the sincere, sensible, affectionate pouring out of the heart or soul to God, through Christ, in the strength and assistance of the Holy Spirit, for such things as God has promised, or according to the Word of God, for the good of the Church, with submission in faith to the will of God.[1]

Prayer demands sincerity, authenticity, a lack of hypocrisy. No duplicity is allowed. It must be rational, rooted in Biblical truth and spiritual reality. It must involve the heart, the pouring out of the inner self. Passion is demanded. It was said that John Fletcher, author and pastor, stained the walls of his room by the breath of his prayer. He would pray all night, with earnestness. He asked when greeting others, "Do I meet you praying?"[2]

The often colorful Vance Havner declared, "The same church members who yell like Comanche Indians at a ball game on Sat-

What is Prayer?

urday sit like wooden Indians in church on Sunday." Yet, prayer is neither a fervent effort of flesh or will, nor a self-control exercise based on Christian logic. Good praying demands divine partnership accomplished only by the strength and assistance of God, the Holy Spirit. It is bound to Biblical promises and principles. It rises above the temporal, the earthly, and touches eternal kingdom purposes. It is offered in faith, yet with submission to God's will. It is, as Henri Nouwen noted,

> ...no easy matter. It demands a relationship in which you allow the other to enter into the very center of your person, to speak there, to touch the sensitive core of your being, and allow the other to see so much that you would rather leave in darkness.[3]

I had been involved in ministry for over 25 years when I admitted to God that I didn't understand prayer. Involved in the prayer summit movement, I spent days at retreat centers with pastors of almost every denomination. We prayed morning, noon and night. We encountered God. I was immeasurably enriched and forever changed. I had found the heart of ministry – the pursuit of His presence. Still, I longed to understand the workings of prayer.

My quest ultimately sent me back to Scripture; specifically, to the *prayers of the Bible*.[4] Those prayers provided insights that radically changed my perspective. Prayer, I discovered, wasn't fundamentally "asking of God" – *petition*. Nor was the center of prayer passionate *intercession*. It wasn't simply "talking to God" or engaging in any one of a host of other valuable prayer functions[5] – meditation, supplication, beseeching, crying out, petition, adoration, confession, thanksgiving, praise, supplication and more. Prayer involves discerning, wrestling, resting, pulling-down, rooting-out, warfare, reconciliation, agreement, watching, resting, hearing and obeying. It encompasses all of these, but it is more than even the sum total of these components.

THREE ASPECTS OF PRAYER

Prayer can be most simply understood in three categories – *communion, petition* and *intercession*. All these are wrapped in a fourth – *thanksgiving*. This is Paul's theology of prayer (1 Tim. 2:1).

- ♦ *Communion* is the heart of prayer with God.
- ♦ *Petition* is asking things of God, making requests, and is possible only because of the communal relationship we have with the Father through Jesus (John 14:13; 15:16; 16:23, 26).
- ♦ *Intercession* is the position in the middle. It involves our duty as believers to pray for others, particularly those who lack a vital, saving relationship with Christ. But that is possible only because we ourselves are in such a redeemed relationship. Out of communion, we intercede.
- ♦ *Thanksgiving* is the overflow of a heart that recognizes what a gift God has given to us though Christ. We are grateful and we say so to God in front of others.

So, if the heart of prayer is *communion* with God, how do we enter into such communion?

What is Prayer?

Communion with God Is More Than Meditation

Quiet reflection is increasingly viewed as being synonymous with Biblical prayer. But prayer is not simply reflectively and deductively thinking your way through some crisis or life decision, even if that process acknowledges God.

Eastern meditation is currently an American rage, but its focus is the subjective inner self. It calls for you to *empty* your mind. Christian meditation is different: it is objective, focused on Christ, His character, and His life in us (Psalm 1:1-3). It calls for you to *fill* your mind with Christ and with Scripture. Rather than search for strength and answers from *within*, Biblical prayer calls us *out of ourselves*. Wisdom to solve life's complex problems and the power to triumph over them is not called out through the focused spiritual reflection of the inner self. Christian prayer accepts our weakness, inadequacy and our frailty. It reaches *beyond our self* and to God – so large that the ever-expanding universe is too small for Him.

Prayer and Scripture go hand in hand. We hear God through the conduit of Scripture. Memorization and meditation write Scripture on the inner walls of our heart. They inform our prayer life. In their light, we see things from heaven's perspective. Christian meditation uses the lens of Scripture. When hidden in our hearts (Psalm 119:11), it creates inner reference points that cause a confident recognition of His will and way and a sharpened sense of discernment (John 14:26).

Christ-centered mediation is a powerful means of quieting the soul. It stills the heart and shuts out the noisy world. It positions us to clearly hear God. But meditation cannot take the place of verbal prayer. Jesus says, *"When you pray, say..."* He intended that we would *speak*. That we would pray *aloud*.

Communion with God Demands Speech

A man who believes that *thinking* he loves his spouse is the same as *saying,* "I love you! Forgive me," is greatly mistaken. Hosea told Israel, "<u>*Take with you words,*</u> *and turn to the Lord: <u>say</u> to Him, 'Take away all iniquity and receive us graciously'*" (Hosea 14:2). Prayer involves intentional, verbal speech. *Thinking something* is not the same as *praying* it.

God created man with the capacity for speech. The Biblical God is a *speaking* God. He could have willed the universe by thought. Instead, He *spoke* it into existence. The capacity for speech sets the human species apart. It is a divine-like quality. *"Life and death,"* the Scripture says, *"is in the power of the tongue."* (Proverbs 18:21) In prayer, we declare God's life over death-like situations. We prophetically call for victory in situations that appear hopeless. Prayer is a life-altering force.

This is not to suggest that our speech, in the form of prayer or the prophetic, has original creative energy. Words are powerful but only God's speech is *omnipotent.* Borrowing Biblical language, our speech is *potent, but not omnipotent.* Really powerful moments come when our voice joins God's voice; when we echo heaven's will on the earth. We express into our time-space world what God is saying from His throne in heaven. Spirit-quickened prayers lend our human voice to His Divine voice. Make no mistake. Bible-based, Spirit-led prayerful speech is powerful. "God governs by the prayers of his people," great prayer leaders observe. The alignment of heaven and earth by prayer sets off global changes.

Communion with God Is Praying Beyond Words

Something happens when thoughts are spoken even alone in prayer. Someone has said, "A word is a thought eternalized!"[6] The experience of hearing ourselves saying a certain thing has an affect

What is Prayer?

that thought alone does not produce. And yet, prayer is beyond words. It is

> ...deeper than words. The total content of the all the prayers of Jesus can be repeated in less than 15 minutes. Prayer is present in the soul before it has been formulated in words. And it abides in the soul after the last words of prayer have passed over our lips.[7]

You really haven't prayed until you have prayed yourself to silence. Pour out your soul and declare confidence in God, His love for you and your love and allegiance to Him. Wrestle with the will of God. Then submit, declaring that you are at peace with the assertion of His will in the matter. In such moments, there are no more words to be said. Ole Kristian Hallesby observed:

> **Prayer is the highest use to which speech can be put.**
> **– P. T. Forsyth**

> There comes times when I have nothing more to tell God. If I were to continue to pray in words, I would have to repeat what I have already said. At such times it is wonderful to say to God, "May I be in Thy presence, Lord? I have nothing more to say to Thee, but I do love to be in Thy presence."[8]

A sweet and searing silence laces your heart to the heart of God. You know that He loves you and He knows that you deeply love Him. You sense that He has heard. An "everything-is-going-to-be-alright" peace comes. Jonathan Edwards describes the effect of such prayer:

> My sense of divine things gradually increased, and became more and more lively, and had more...inward sweetness. The appearance of every thing was altered; there seemed to be, as it were a calm, sweet cast, or appearance of divine glory, in almost everything.
>
> God's excellency, his wisdom, his purity and love seemed to appear in everything; in the sun, moon, and stars; in the clouds, and blue sky; in the grass, flowers, trees; in the water, and all nature...singing forth, with a low voice my contemplations of the Creator and Redeemer...[9]

At the start, prayer *demands* words. You *talk* with God. You passionately describe your situation, your perspective, your needs and more. Scriptural language will enlarge your capacity to express your heart. You pray in the Spirit. But in the end, you will discover language alone cannot express your heart. Words are vessels that help empty the cargo of the soul. Deeper levels of prayer are impossible without this emptying. Then on the other side of words, you come to the sweetest level of prayer. John Bunyan said, "In prayer, it is better to have heart without words, than words without heart." This is communion with God. It is the heart of prayer.

Communion with God Is Unity with the Spirit

Prayer produces its ultimate state when the Spirit seamlessly reveals Christ to us and through us. He prays for us. Through us He speaks. We give voice to the Spirit, praying as God would have us pray, until as yielded vessels even the tongue, the unruly member, is in perfect submission. There is congruence, inner harmony. An *"all is well, God is on His throne"* disposition governs. We are centered in God's love. Brother Lawrence says the essence of prayer is *this sense of His presence*.[10]

WHY GOD WANTS US TO PRAY

J. Sidlow Baxter declared, "No blessing of the Christian life becomes continually possessed unless we are men and women of regular, daily, unhurried secret lingering in prayer."[11] For some "prayer is a form of spiritual gambling: you make your needs and desires known and hope for the best."[12] Others ask, "Why should we pray? God knows what we need before we ask?" (Matthew 6:8). Some believe that God, out of goodness alone, will automatically take care of their needs. He cares for the birds of the air and lilies of the field. Will He not automatically take care of us? The answer is a surprising, *"No!"*

What is Prayer?

"You have not," James told us, *"because you ask not"* (James 4:2). You must pray. God has subordinated supply to prayer. It is the process by which the believer appropriates heaven's resources out of the estate of Christ. God could act apart from prayer, but He chooses to act in connection with prayer. Prayer is always the place to start with our needs. James asks needy believers, *"Why don't you pray?"* (James 4:2). Evidently, the Christians there had prayed (4:3), but God didn't answer. Their motives were wrong. They were praying for selfish reasons. God refuses to answer prayers that deepen our bondage to self. His goal is to liberate us and transform us.

God Loves Company

The Christians to whom James was writing had come to see prayer only as a means of acquisition. God is more than the clerk of heaven's storehouse. He wants a relationship with us. That is extraordinary! The Greek gods were a self-centered lot. World religions are full of gods that are indifferent or so transcendent that they are unknowable. In Christianity, God becomes a friend to man. He can be known. He walks and talks with us. He is moved with the feeling of our infirmities. Search the faiths of the world and you will find no other God like this One!

God wants company. He created man with a capacity for fellowship. After Creation, He came walking through the garden looking for Adam. From Genesis to Jesus, we have a friendly, talking God. Prayer is the means by which He fellowships with us. Prayer is relational. And relationships necessitate communication. But deep relationships extend beyond language to a wordless connection possible only after all that needs to be said has been said. In prayer, we find the acceptance and affirmation of God.

God relates to us, loves us, likes us, encourages and nurtures us, directs and warns us, convicts and corrects us, grows and develops us. All of this happens in the context of prayer.

Prayer Is A Privilege

The very privilege of Christian prayer is such a precious gift that we hardly understand how extraordinary it is. We take it for granted! We assume that all people pray and understand it in similar ways. A Muslim must pray in Arabic, but he is never sure that Allah hears. A Hindu must seek the services of a Brahman to do his praying for him. Buddhism teaches that we are to embrace suffering, to not expect an answer. The Buddhist must save himself.

Who do we think we are that we can ask *God to serve us?* That we are granted the *right* to a hearing in His courtroom? That at times, He may command heaven to respond to some aspect of our request? Christian prayer is astoundingly different to the prayer of other religions, and we are often blind to its noble character. We are so blessed! We may not only approach the throne of the King of the universe, the Creator and Sovereign, but are told to do so with boldness. Such an act is unthinkably laden with grace. Christian prayer – what a rare privilege!

In the Old Testament, Israel knew God as a Father, but no individual called him "*my* Father!" The New Testament perspective is so wonderfully different. We stand on the Resurrection side of time. Christ has died and risen, rescuing the Old Testament saints from death's prison. He is on the throne in heaven. The Father, in answer to his prayer, has sent the Holy Spirit who lives in our hearts. We have been given the privilege of prayer in his name. We call God "Father," through our relationship with Christ! Sealed and indwelt by the Spirit, we are afforded the opportunity to live in unbroken fellowship with God.

From Pluto, the sun is a dim light appearing like a distant star in a perpetual night sky. All is dark and cold. The long journey around the sun takes 247.7 Earth years. A day on Pluto is 6.39 earth years.[13] In contrast, from Earth, the sun is no distant star. Its orange glow fills our sky daily. Its heat warms us. Its light chases the darkness away. How wonderful to live in the light of the New Testament. No longer distant, because of Christ, a new closeness with God is possible. We may now approach the Throne and fellowship with the light. And yet, there is also in the 'Lord's Prayer' a hint at the Father's transcendence, not explicit, but implicit. Our Father who 'art' – He is transcendent, in eternity, beyond time. Our Father in 'heaven' – He is in another dimension, beyond the confining bounds of space. He is not spatially distant, but transcendent - outside of time and space. Our Father 'hallowed' – He is utterly other, different than.

Prayer is Heaven's Way of Blessing

Andrew Murray says,

God's intense longing to bless is graciously limited by his dependence upon intercession. God regards intercession as the highest expression of our readiness to participate wholly and fully in the working of his will. [14]

"God's intense longing to bless!" What a concept! According to Murray, God not only *longs* to bless, He *intensely longs* to bless. But that "longing to bless," Murray continues "is limited!" How could any intense longing of the Sovereign God be limited? "It is graciously limited by His dependence on intercession." That is, God could act apart from prayer, but He chooses not to do so.

Murray says, "God regards intercession as the highest expression of our readiness to participate fully and completely in the working of His will." Prayer invites God's involvement in our world. And by the use of its processes, it changes us. It readies us to more fully partner with God. Our prayerlessness breaks the heart of God. Remedies for all our problems are a prayer away. Our lack of prayer keeps us in need. It frustrates our participation in the will of God. What blessings we are missing by our prayerlessness.

Prayer Taps the Bounty in the Endowment of Christ

Imagine that your parents have a house packed full of family treasures you desire. To take them while they are alive would be unthinkable – theft. Even at the tragic news of their death, to race to their house to claim the best of their possessions would be in bad taste, perhaps even illegal, especially if they have a will. A will is a legal document, supported by the court system and all its police power. The whole authority of the State stands behind the enforcement of a legal will.

Through a will, one can control the distribution of what they acquired even after they are gone. You are an heir. You have an inheritance traceable to Christ – a wealth of treasures. The writer of Hebrews reminds us that *"a will and testament is valid only when the maker of the will dies"* (Hebrews 9:16-17). When Christ died, He left an expressed will. The New Testament is His last will. He continues to exercise distribution rights to his heirs.

Prayer's Basis of Appeal – Covenant Promises

The only way you and I have a claim on the estate of Christ, the promises of God, is through the court of heaven by our covenant relationship with Jesus Christ (Hebrews 9:18-20; 12:23-24; Matthew 28:16). There is no other basis for appeal in any courtroom apart from law! Grace answered the law and satisfied its demands (Ephesians 2:1-8). So, it is our covenant that gives us the privilege of prayer, of accessing the throne of God (Romans 5:1-3). We can file a petition, a claim on the storehouses of heaven, based on the finished work of Christ.

By prayer, we enter heaven's courtroom and draw from the riches of the estate of Christ (Ephesians 3:8; Philippians 4:19). The Holy Spirit is our counselor and the executor of the estate. Jesus said, *"All that the Father has is Mine..."* (John 16:15). And, *"He [the Holy Spirit] will take the things of Mine and reveal them unto you..."* (John 16:13-15). The Father, the Judge Himself, decrees the allocations (John 15:16; 16:23).

Paul tells us that it is the Holy Spirit who distributes gifts (1 Corinthians 12:7, 11). These could be called "gracious bestowments." Out of grace, he divides them severally as he wills. We are heirs, joint-heirs with Christ (Romans 8:17; Titus 3:7; Hebrews 6:17; James 2:5). Praying and wishing are not the same. We pray according to Biblical principles, informed by Scriptural insight, aligning ourselves with the will and ways of God as revealed in the sacred writings, specifically, the New Testament. Our prayers lay claim to the promises of God in Christ. We have no other basis on which we might ask for God anything. Prayer demands an open Bible. Many Christians are wishing, not praying, which, based on the principles and promises of Scripture, leads us to "pray amiss."

Prayer Invites the Kingdom of God

Jesus taught what we commonly call "the Lord's Prayer!" In truth, it is the disciples' prayer. In Matthew 6:9, it is a model, a template for prayer *("In this manner...pray!")*. In Luke 11:2, it is a form, a prayer to be prayed repeatedly. Actually, it is both. A form to be repeated as the prayer of our heart; and a model of the way we should pray.[15] Never once in this prayer do you find – *me, my* or *I*. Instead you find – *our, us* and *we*. Prayer cannot be about our narrow slice of pain. It pulls us out of our little world. In this prayer, we request that His exiled kingdom break into our time-space world, *"Thy kingdom come."* This expresses dissidence in the face of the rising darkness and our declaration of allegiance to His rejected kingship. We plead for His will to be done; *"thy will be done on earth as in heaven."* His rule asserted. And for His name to be 'hallowed,' treated respectfully, as holy.

This prayer begins and ends with the Kingdom. This is the overall purpose of all prayer – to bring the earth, beginning with us, under His lordship. As the agents of this Kingdom, we are to be different from the world around us. We are dependent upon His hand for daily bread. We are a forgiving people, as we have been forgiven. We are a holy people who do not want to be led into temptation or overpowered with evil desire. Here is the heart of Christianity: faith for the day; love for others; and purity in life. And yet saying this prayer is not the same as praying it.

Superstitious repetition is a pagan notion which Jesus warned against (Matthew 6:7). Prayer should borrow its words and form from Scripture, but ultimately, it has to rise from the heart. The Jewish Rabbis taught "Index Prayers." These were abbreviated outlines for prayer. They were single phrases to be memorized as a track for prayer. Each phrase suggested an item for more extensive and spontaneous prayer. The purpose was to create a focus for prayer. We are so easily distracted.

The prayer that Jesus taught appears to be an "Index Prayer!"[16] We pray it and expand it extemporaneously, inspired by the Spirit, use its ideas for our own heart-felt prayer. We pray out of the prayer, creating a personalized and expanded version. Drawing from the language of Scripture, we enlarge our capacity for expression, always making the prayer our own. Remember, however, form will never take the place of fire. Nor can mere language or prayer phrases take the place of deep yearning.

What is Prayer?

FOREWORD

1. Chuck Swindoll, *So, You Want To Be Like Christ?* (Nashville, TN: W Publishing Group, a division of Thomas Nelson, 2005), 61-62.
2. Swindoll, 100.

CHAPTER ONE

1. John Bunyan, "True Prayer," *The Contemporaries Meet The Classics on Prayer*, ed. Leonard Allen (West Monroe, LA: Howard Publishing, 2003), 15.
2. E. M. Bounds, *Power through Prayer* (Worldwide Publications, 1989), 45.
3. Henri Nouwen, "Resistance to Prayer." *The Contemporaries Meet The Classics on Prayer*, ed. Leonard Allen (West Monroe, LA: Howard Publishing, 2003), 151.
4. For an extensive listing, see Lockyer, *All the Prayers of the Bible* (Grand Rapids, MI: Zondervan, 1959).
5. See *The Praying Church Resource Guide*, Section 3 for definitions of each of these prayer functions. P. Douglas Small, *The Praying Church Resource Guide* (Kannapolis, NC: Alive Publications, 2013).
6. O. Hallesby. <ezinearticles.com/?Harness-The-Power-Of-Words-In-Your-Life&id=57618>.
7. O. Hallesby. *Prayer* (Minneapolis, MN: Augsburg Publishing, 1931), 16.
8. O. Hallesby. <www.quotegarden.com/prayer.html>.
9. Jonathan Edwards, "Vehement Longings After God," *The Contemporaries Meet The Classics on Prayer*, ed. Leonard Allen (West Monroe, LA: Howard Publishing, 2003), 99.
10. Brother Lawrence, *The Practice of the Presence of God.* (New York: Fleming H. Revell Company, 1958), See also: <www.prayerfoundation.org/booktexts/z_brother_lawrence_001_index.htm>.
11. <www.famousquotesandauthors.com/topics/prayer_quotes.html>.
12. George Barna, *The Index of Leading Spiritual Indicators* (Word Publications, 1996), 23.
13. <www.enchantedlearning.com/subjects/astronomy/planets/pluto/ - 26k>.
14. Herbert Lockyer, *All the Prayers of the Bible* (Grand Rapids, MI: Zondervan, 1959), 5.
15. Arthur W. Pink, *A Guide to Fervent Prayer* (Baker Publishing Group, 1995), 72.
16. Herbert Lockyer, 192.

CHAPTER 2
What Prayer Says About God

Prayer is often defined as our talking to God. It does involve words. In this conversation with God, He hears us perfectly, but we struggle to hear His voice clearly. Consequently, prayer is reduced to *our* talking to God, *our telling* God what we desire or what we would like to see Him do in this or that matter.

BACK TO THE BEGINNING

One key principle in understanding the Bible is to go back to the first mention of the idea in the Bible. So, let's go back to Genesis and look for prayer. The first two encounters between God and man are Genesis 1:28-30 and 2:16-17. In both encounters, God does all the talking and man is silent. God initiates an encounter with man - twice.[1] And then, even after man's sin, God again initiates an interaction, in fact, with man avoiding Him.

It's fascinating isn't it, that so early in Scripture, we meet prayer avoidance. But also, here we find God's grace. After man sins, when he has violated the very boundaries about which he was warned, God still comes to him to talk. He repairs the relational breach with a sacrifice (3:21). He covers man. He corrects. Yet, He doesn't spare him all the consequences – sin has damaged man's strategic dominion (Gen. 3:17-19). It has injured the marriage relationship – both Adam and Eve are hiding, not only from God, but one another. The split created by sin is both vertical – Godward; and horizontal – between the couple. God acts, so as to not allow sin to completely sever the relationship. What grace! Then and now, grace is the ground on which prayer takes place.

Looking at the passage, it's clear that God wants communion with man more than man desires communion with Him. No other faith offers such a God! A pursing God. A blessing God. An empowering God. A disciplining God. A restoring God. Such a gracious God.

God Wants to Talk to You

The idea that God speaks to people is met with ridicule today, even in Christian circles. In fact, some see the idea as dangerous. So prayer then, to make it safe, is reduced to an inner conversation. It is redefined as sanctified self-talk. But that is not the picture the Bible presents. Jesus promises, *"My sheep hear my voice!"* (John 10:3-4, 16, 27). He explains that, the Holy Spirit will teach you. *"But when he, the Spirit of truth, comes, he will guide you into all the truth. He will not speak on his own; he will speak only what he hears, and he will tell you what is yet to come"* (John 16:13).

Jesus expected us to receive the Holy Spirit, to be directed by the Spirit, and to hear from heaven. He expected Spirit disclosures to impact our future and our decisions, to help us see around the curves of life. The New Living Translation says, *"He will tell you about the future."* The ESV says, *"he will not speak on his own authority, but whatever he hears [in heaven] he will speak."* Prayer then allows us to hear echoes of heaven, the repeated whispers from another world. Jesus, in prayer, through the Spirit, *"will de-*

clare to you the things that are to come." The Aramaic Bible in Plain English says bluntly, *"he will lead you into the whole truth...and he shall reveal the future to you."*

God expects us to hear His voice, by the indwelling, in-filling Holy Spirit. This sometimes happens as the words of Scripture leap off the page and come alive with new meaning. Whatever the means, God, speaks to His people.

What God is Saying

In these first encounters between God and man in Genesis 1:28 and 2:16-17, we have noted, it is God who takes the initiative. Man sins, man says nothing, only God speaks. What did God say? And what is He saying now – to you and me?

God's first message to man was the pronouncing of a blessing! *"Then God blessed them and said, 'Be fruitful and multiply. Fill the earth and govern it. Reign over the fish in the sea, the birds in the sky, and all the animals that scurry along the ground'"* (Gen. 1:28).

Notice the content of the blessing, the scope of this blessing – fruitfulness at a multiplying level, a global mission, governance, empowerment, stewardship. The breadth and reach of this blessing is stunning. It is not narrow, by any means. It points to the confidence God has in Adam, to God's free sharing of authority and trust. Here is the strategic positioning of mankind.

The 'law of the first mention' is a principle for Biblical interpretation. It means that the first occurrence of a subject in Scripture is often instructive, setting a trajectory. This is a powerful blessing. Could the purpose of prayer be for God to bless us? Not in a narrow self-interested way, but to position us for service and ministry? Even for success? Here, God says to Adam and Eve, *"Be fruitful,"* not barren. To them, He gives the power of procreative life – something He withheld from angels. He gives them responsibility for the earth, but He also gives the gift of dominion over the earth. This is empowerment, and it is virtually limitless potential. *"Have dominion over the whole earth!"* It is an incredible global mission – *"over the sea, and the land, and the air."*

Prayer and Blessing

The word 'bless' in Hebrew means *knee*. It implies the posture of kneeling. To pray is to kneel before God. To kneel before God in prayer is to put oneself in the position of being blessed by God. We learn later, in the case of Jacob and Esau, that a blessing's power is not released until it is spoken (Genesis 27:33, 22-38). And when it is spoken, it is enduring.

In Genesis, we have Adam and Eve kneeling before God and receiving a blessing, one spoken over them. It is, in effect, their wedding ceremony, with God presiding. *"And he blessed them,"* not at the level of addition, but of multiplication. Not to survive, but to thrive. Not to live in some level of guarded fear in the vast earth but to take on the task of dominion. This is breathtaking.

What blessing are you missing by prayerlessness? What narrow benefit are you attempting to wrestle from the hand of God, perceiving of prayer as your need list, and never quieting yourself, kneeling reverently, to have Him bless you with an empowering affirmation of His will and desire for you? Have you and your spouse ever knelt before God, and asked Him to bless the two of you, your marriage and family, your home and business?

We *"have not, because we ask not,"* that is, because we don't pray. Prayer here is simply putting oneself in the position to be blessed. And the nature of God, it seems, is not tight-fisted and resistant, but benevolent and generous. Does God want to bless you in some stunning way that you have missed by seeing prayer so narrowly, so one-sided? Have you waited before Him?

The second encounter with man is a gracious warning (Gen. 2:16-17). Heightened sensitivity should also come through prayer. The first encounter is God blessing. In the second, God sets a boundary. *"Of every tree you may eat, but of the tree of the knowledge of good and evil, you may not eat..."* The boundary is to protect the blessing. Prayer itself is a kind of boundary for daily spiritual orientation. It priortizes our need. Without such a boundary, we lose the blessing. Without the daily discipline of prayer, our life lacks a definitive moment of consecration to God. Such an act redeems time. It marks a time to be with God. In that way, it protects our relationship with God. Prayer creates holy space. It says to God, "I need your blessing. I want to hear your voice. I want to obey and do your will."

Heightening Spiritual Sensitivity

There is in prayer, a kind of heightening of spiritual sensitivity. Prayer tunes our hearts to hear God more clearly. God said to Jeremiah, *"Call to me [pray] and I will answer you, and will tell you great and hidden things that you have not known"* (33:3). God promises not only to answer, but as Jeremiah and Jesus told us, that the answer would be about *"great and hidden things"* we would not otherwise know. Prayer discloses. To Elijah, God spoke in a still small voice (1 Kings 19:12). God told the prophet Isaiah, *"...your ears shall hear a word behind you, saying, 'This is the way, walk in it,' when you turn to the right or when you turn to the left"* (30:21).

Jesus promised, *"Whenever you are arrested and brought to trial, do not worry beforehand about what to say. Just say whatever is given you at the time, for it is not you speaking, but the Holy Spirit"* (Mark 13:11; also Matthew 10:20 and Luke 12:12). In such moments, not only are we assured the passive presence of God, but his active speaking. The power of the blessing is found not in merely

The Fall of Man and the Serpent

In Genesis 3:14-15, we read, *"And the Lord God said to the serpent, 'Because you have done this, cursed are you more than all cattle, more than every beast of the field; on your belly shall you go and dust shall you eat all the days of your life. And I will put enmity between you and the woman, between your seed and her seed. He shall bruise you on the head, and you shall bruise him on the heel."* Here is a divine curse, upon the serpent, and by extension, on Satan. Of course, man and woman also taste the consequences of sin (v. 16-18).

Erwin Lutzer, in his book, *The Serpent of Paradise*, tells the story of a contractor who submitted a bid on a multi-million-dollar project. On the last day to submit bids, he walked into the office of the general contractor and found it empty. On the desk was the bid of one of his competitors. Covering the bottom-line, the actual bid amount, was a can of soda. If, he reasoned, he knew that amount, he could alter his bid and be assured of winning the job. As he waited, and no one entered the office, the temptation to look at the bid intensified. Confident that he was alone, he lifted the can, ever so slightly, to peep at the bottom-line number. As he tilted the soda can, small BBs rolled across the desk and tumbled onto the floor. His willingness to taint the process, to win by dishonesty, was manifest. The unintended consequences he experienced went far beyond the private moment. Things were not as they appeared.

The fall set in motion an avalanche of unintended consequences. It garnered a 'curse.'[1] And, a curse is far more than sin's mere

---

[1] Three Hebrew verbs (*'alah, 'arar, and qalal*) can be translated "curse." The terms can be applied to oaths, imprecations (judgment words), maledictions (the opposite of a benediction, a blessing), and they are used in covenant formulas, and in which case, they may be condition or unconditional. They are meant as power words. Though humans may curse, the great concern, as in Genesis, is when God curses. The attempted curse of Balaam, the prophet, under God's sovereignty, morphed into blessing (Numbers 22-24). Blessing and curse are His property. In Genesis 3:14, the curse on the serpent was a judgment curse. The bottom line is the sovereignty and moral management of God in our world. He gets the final word with regard to right and wrong, good and bad, what is to be blessed and what is to be cursed. See: Brian M. Britt, "Curses in the Hebrew Bible", n.d. [cited 30 Oct 2016]. Online: www.bibleodyssey.org:443/en/people/related-articles/curses-in-the-hebrew-bible

hearing God's word, but in the trust and obedience that follow: *"Blessed rather are those who hear the word of God and keep it!"* (Luke 11:28). Without obedience, we lose the blessing.

In a confrontational moment with the Pharisees, Jesus argued forcibly, *"Whoever is of God hears the words of God. The reason why you do not hear them is that you are not of God"* (John 8:47). By rejecting Jesus, they were rejecting the Father. Hearing God means hearing Jesus – he is 'Word' become flesh. *"My sheep,"* Jesus said, *"hear my voice, and I know them, and they follow me"* (John 10:27). And other sheep, *"not of this fold,"* not Jewish, *"I must bring them also, and they will listen to my voice."* The indicator that Jews or Gentiles are in the fold of Jesus, and are truly 'his sheep,' is a prayer relationship – they are hearing 'my voice' (John 10:16).

Paul offered a simple marker for those who were 'sons of God,' namely, they *"are led by the Spirit of God"* (Romans 8:14). The faith that comes by 'hearing the word of God' is not found in passively listening to preaching. The English Standard Version makes the slight but important distinction, *"...faith comes from hearing, and hearing through the word of Christ"* (Romans 10:17). This is not natural hearing. It is not merely hearing a sermon or teaching. It is hearing – by and through another medium, *"the word of Christ."* The Aramaic Bible in Plain English says that *"faith is from the hearing ear, and the hearing ear is from the word..."* It is more than the ear, since, *"The natural person does not accept the things of the Spirit of God... he is not able to understand them,"* and the reason is simple – *"they are spiritually discerned"* (1 Corinthians 2:14). As you pray, especially over an open Bible, *"the eyes of your heart,"* not merely those of your head, will *"be enlightened"* (Ephesians 1:18). Hope will grow as will your awareness of being made 'rich' by 'his glorious inheritance'. The NLT says, *"your hearts will be flooded with light so that you can understand the confident hope he has given to those he called."* The Holman Christian Standard Bible says, consequences. It essentially recalibrated the dimensions of the earlier blessing, removing certain components, adding inevitable pain to the process. It is consequential and specifically judicial.

Here is divine judgment. Sin is not only a violation of God's moral law; His law is an extension of His essence, His character. Sin, then, is a personal affront to God. It is an act of war against the nature of God. It is an affront to His sovereignty, His right to say what is 'good and bad'. And further, it is a form of differentiation from God, choosing other than God would choose, walking away from and apart from God and His wisdom – it is divisive. It violates the moral order of God, rebels against His sovereignty, and stands apart from Him, also creating a rift in relational order. The 'apple' aside, what was underneath the sin of mankind, motivating him, destroyed paradise.

In the end, God's holiness (moral order), His authority (sovereign order) and His unity (relational order) were not threatened. Man fell, not God. Satan, in the symbol of the serpent, does not improve his rank or status before or against God. Here, he loses ground, being the victim of a curse. He advances his hold over mankind, through their weakness to sin, but God is not diminished. There is no contest that by necessity involves our God with Lucifer. He is not an equal, as darkness is no equal to light. The struggle of humanity with sin and Satan has been heightened by the fall, but the fact of the curse, here, is an indication that even upon Satan, there are limits imposed by God's judicial sovereignty.

In Genesis 3:14, "God said to the serpent" – the reptile, "Because you have done this, cursed are you more than all cattle, more than every beast of the field; on your belly shall you go and dust shall you eat all the days of your life." He has been a tool of Satan, perhaps not even a willing or rational partner. While that may seem severe, it reinforces God's sovereignty, and may serve to set a boundary, going forward, of Satan's use of Earth's creatures. It may be a line of grace affecting the whole animal world. To the serpent, as an example to all creation, "Because you were the instrument in the temptation of man, cursed are you..."

"the perception of your mind may be enlightened." And that heightens hope and confidence. God speaks to us, and in doing so, He enlightens us. That strengthens hope and confidence.

Our prayerful encounters with God, over Scripture, also cause us to discover that the Bible is a living book, transformed into an animated sword. At times, it cuts us. It pierces deeply into our hearts. What is dull to others, reading the Bible, we find the quite the opposite, discovering that *"the word of God is living and active"* (Hebrews 4:12). It engages us, penetrating our souls. In those piercing moments, God's voice sometimes wounds like a sword, separating our thoughts (soul) from the those of the Spirit. Here, deep discernment is found, and the thoughts and intents of our hearts are examined and parsed for purity and clarity (Hebrews 4:12).

Seeing Prayer's Bigger Purpose

Prayer both invites God's blessing, and by grace, it sets boundaries. It heightens discernment, helping us to preserve that blessing by warnings, intuitive hunches, spiritual discernment, a word of knowledge or wisdom, sometimes in the form of a scripture, and at other times, a vague awareness of our need to be on guard.

The Natural or the Spiritual

Oswald Chambers says the first temptation was not about good and evil. This is why we are mystified at the terrible consequences of the first couple's act of pulling an apple from the one tree God had forbidden. How could stealing an 'apple' cause the world to tumble into darkness? The idea seems strange to us; it doesn't resonate. In fact, God appears as a crabby orchard keeper, acting worse than Adam and Eve.

Chambers says that the fall did not occur on the continuum of good and evil; there was no evil in the heart of man. He was

When God spoke to the serpent, he had more than the reptile in mind. He was also speaking to Satan.[2] The curse on the serpent is a reminder of God's degradation of Satan, who is represented in biblical literature as a serpent (Rev. 12:9; 20:2). This is quite a fall, for Lucifer was once the 'anointed cherub' of heaven. In his first fall, he lost his position in heaven (Isa. 14:12). And here, in his seduction of humanity, he experiences a further restraint. "On your belly shall you go and the dust shall you eat all the days of your life." The humiliated, crawling, slithering, dust-bound serpent illustrates the curse. When the lion lies down with the lamb and the carnivorous nature of the animal world is removed, the effect of sin's curse will be lifted from all creatures – cattle and every beast of the field – but the serpent will continue to eat dust (Gen. 3:14; Isa. 65:25). Likewise, the curse will never lift from Lucifer. His position will never improve, only degenerate.

Satan *appears* as something he is not. He is a master at disguise, presenting himself, for example, as an angel of light (2 Cor. 11:14). He moves through the Earth 'like a roaring lion,' ready to eat us alive (1 Pet. 5:8), but heaven sees him as a lowly, slithering snake. He has power, no doubt, but 'the curse' is an indicator that his power, though formidable when used as deception and accusation (Rev. 12:9-10), is limited. It has on it restraint, by God's sovereign, judicial decree. He may claim to be Earth's sovereign, due to the default of man, but the Earth remains the Lord's (Psa. 24:1; 1 Cor. 10:26). Satan's reign is an illusion.

From the woman will come One who will crush the head of the already debased Serpent. In the meantime, there will be 'enmity' between humanity and the serpent – that is, he might attempt to dominate the earth, but his attempts will be resisted, particularly by the people of the seed. God will have a lineage, going forward, a righteous seed, through whom the Messiah will come (Lk. 3:38, 23-38). The easy manner in which Eve and Adam had been duped at the tree would not happen going forward – this is grace, it is the restraint of God on the Evil One. It is enmity between humanity and Satan. Sin had placed enmity between God and the couple; now God imposes it between humanity and Satan, as well. They had avoided God, due to sin, but not the serpent. Now, he scripts into their nature an avoidance of the Serpent.

---

2   This is often called, in prophetic hermeneutics, the law of the double reference.

innocent. Rather, the temptation took place on the continuum of the spiritual and the natural. Would Adam and Eve make decisions from the perspective of the natural or the spiritual? To which world would they be attuned? They chose the natural world – with fruit that was pleasant to the eyes, that seemed desirable, and that they deduced, with help from the Serpent, would make them gods.

Prayer cannot be a matter of wrestling with worldly needs. It is intended to heighten our sensitivity to the world on top of this world, to help us see not the temporal, but the eternal; not the thing that will satisfy now, but the thing that will give eternal life.

Triggering Discernment

We do not know what the tree of life looked like – or if it could be seen with natural eyes at all. We do know that Adam failed to observe the boundary God had set, even after he had been warned. And the consequence was an immediate wedge between humanity and God, and between the first couple. He violated the boundary, and lost the blessing. He failed at imposing on himself discipline, and lost the delightful garden. He attempted to access the spiritual, through the natural and the result was spiritual blindness. Even after conversion, we *"see through a glass darkly"* (1 Cor. 13:12, cf. John 12:40; 2 Cor. 4:4; 1 John 2:10). Adam failed to involve God in the choice. He opened a conversation with the Evil One through the serpent. He failed to engage discernment through prayer.

Coming Out of Hiding

What happens when God blesses, and warns, and we cast aside His warning and disobey? It causes avoidance of God and prayer. There is a great deal of talk today among theologians and philosophers about "divine hiddenness," a phrase that points to God's concealment, His secreted existence, His lack of objective disclosure in life, His silence, especially in the face of disaster and human suffering. The laments in the psalms often charge God with being asleep on the job, not caring, not acting, letting the innocent suffer at the hands of the violent wicked.

The bigger prayer problem is not in God's hiding, it is in our hiding from God. Adam hid. He avoided God. He covered himself physically – we cover ourselves. By covering, we create a presenting self, and we cover the more authentic self, the wounded self, the fearful and sinful self. The biggest problem Christians seem to have is that we hide from God – in church, in life, in sin. We fail to see that prayer demands that we present ourselves to God, openly and honestly, not hiding and avoiding.

God – the Seeker

Even with Adam's avoidance of God, we are given clues about God and His desired relationship with us. Amazingly, God pursues Adam (Gen. 3:9-19). Here we find God's redemptive response to the fall. He wants the relationship more than man; and yet, man needs the relationship more than God. This is the great mystery of prayer. God wants to meet us in prayer, more than we want to meet Him in prayer; and yet, God does not need prayer – we need prayer. So, He pursues us! It is the context in which He blesses and sets boundaries for our protection. It is the place where He redeems and restores after some mistake or fall.

Prayer, then, appropriates God's blessings and honors moral and spiritual boundaries. It should hear and heed God's warnings to perils and dangers that would deny his purposes and cause us to forfeit both blessings and our strategic role. It is then the context in which God redeems mistakes and renews our relationship.

Redemption, indeed, salvation comes through prayer. And it

is God pursuing man, wooing man back to Himself through conviction and redirection. Protection, if we will listen to the voice of God, also comes through prayer, as does blessing and bounty. Do you see prayer as a means of "blessing?" As the means by which God decrees our productivity? Remember, God doesn't add. He multiplies. Do you see prayer as the place where He empowers us – giving victory, enablement? Prayer, it seems, is the gateway to victory, to an overcoming posture in life. In prayer, God offers the kingly status of governance and control. It is not His intention that we face life on earth as victims, but as victors.

Prayer and the God Who Gives

In prayer, God "gives freely" to Adam – all that is in the garden. Is this benevolent, giving God the one to whom you pray? Or do you see God as giving grudgingly? Prayer is the means by which God heightens our moral sensitivities, sets boundaries and issues gracious warnings – that is a gift. When have you left a season of prayer with clear leadings you felt were intended to protect you? When you have sensed God's watchful care, His love for you?

Prayer is God in pursuit, God coming after man – to bless. That's the picture in Genesis. Have you ever felt that God was pursuing you? From the time He saved you, He woke up your sense of His love and care for you, and prayer is the means, the relationship, the on-going conversation, that furthers that love and care of God. At salvation, we came to know grace. We heard God say, "I love you; I forgive you." But that blessing, like that of Adam and Eve, must now be actualized, lived out, experienced. And prayer is the on-going dialogue with God that empowers, redirects, enables us to walk in God's blessing, planted like a tree beside rivers, perpetually fruitful (Psalm 1).

Prayer and the God Who Gives Grace

In Genesis, God refuses to let Adam hide. He refuses to let Adam's failure snuff out the relationship. The pursuing God acts in a redemptive manner. The relationship, though damaged, is salvaged. Just as God refused to let go of Adam and Eve, He refuses to let go of you! What grace!

Adam responded wrongly by shifting the blame (Gen. 3:12) – so do we. You will discover the best approach, the most effective way to come to God, is in total honesty. God knows. He sees. Dishonesty doesn't hide anything from Him. What happens is that we begin to hide our "selves" (Gen. 3:7). We split ourselves in a way that renders us less than authentic. Wholeness demands integrity – especially with God in the privacy of prayer.

Prayer and the God Who Redeems and Disciplines

Earlier we noted that Biblical scholars speak of the 'law of the first mention' of any first subject in Scripture. They look for the added significance, implications that give clues to the importance of some subject, person, place or thing.

If the essence of prayer is an encounter with God and also the context in which God engages us, then the 'law of the first mention' causes us to see Him as the great and gracious initiator. Through prayer, he blesses (1:28), sets boundaries (2:17), and pursues us to redeem us (3:8f). This is prayer – blessing and a trajectory for life; boundaries – borders and lines, cautions and restraints; and then, re-blessing, redeeming, correcting, recalibrating under different conditions.

God will not let us hide from Him or one another. These are the laws of prayer. Blessing comes by prayer – a promise is claimed in prayer, and its blessing appropriated. The Holy Spirit guides and directs us out of prayer, protecting us, protecting our potential, the potential of the blessing. It turns out that blessing is a fragile thing – we can lose it. But prayer is also redemptive. It reclaims, re-centers, redirects, appropriates grace, deals with our shame, and recommissions us. It is the context of reconciliation. It is the context in which God not only summons us, as in Adam and Eve, but he also summoned the serpent.

In this judicial assembly before God, the serpent was dealt with severely for his complicity, as an agent of Satan, in our sin. When we come before God, having sinned, and we are reconciled to God, made right with God, can you imagine that in such moments, Satan is also censored? God cares – even after we sin. And he refuses to allow Satan, our tempter and adversary, to be the rogue agent. He too, is subject to God's courtroom decrees. Here, as an example, his deputy, the serpent, is thoroughly restrained. He is humiliated, reduced to slithering on his belly, a symbol of Satan's diminishment.

Prayer – the Place of Promise and Hope

Prayer then is a place of discipline and of judgment, but also of grace and redemption. It has a prophetic dimension to it. God speaks over Adam and Eve, declaring the consequences of their behavior, but retaining the relationship and promising that the serpent's head would one day be crushed. He wakes them up to the danger of the serpent, putting enmity between the righteous line and the serpent, heightening their discernment. He humiliates the serpent, Satan, openly before the two of them, putting a restraint upon him. He gives grace and hope.

OUR PURSUING GOD

We see prayer as us pursuing God. We pray – and wonder where He is. We ask, and wait, for answers that don't readily come.

But, in truth, we're not the chasers – God is the real chaser! Here in Genesis, God pursues, God talks, God blesses, God sets boundaries, and then He acts to redeem, saving the relationship.

He wants a relationship with you, more than you want one with him. Remember, God is not so much disappointed *with you* when you fail to pray, as he is disappointed *for you!*

---

1   Later, in Genesis 2, man names the animals paraded in front of him by God (2:19-20), and there is the exclamation of Adam, when Eve is presented to him (v. 23). Yet, neither the naming of the animals or the verbal acknowledgement by Adam of Eve's likeness to his own, come close to being like a prayerful exchange between God and man. They in fact, seem to be extensions of prayer – a kind of prophetic-discerning function. Yet, Adam, though engaged by God, never seems to engage with God. Only when Adam is confronted, after his sin, does he respond verbally to God (Gen. 3:10-13). Unfortunately, his confession is partial and distorted. Its essence, like that of the woman's confession that follows, is blame-shifting.

CHAPTER 3
What Prayer Says About Us

The Bible is full of language that shows man pursuing God. *"As the deer pants for streams of water, so I long for you God"* (Psalm 42:1). *"Those who seek me find me"* (Proverbs 8:17). We are urged by Jesus, to ask, seek and knock (Mt. 7:7).

God is Waiting

In Isaiah 65:1, God amazingly says, *"I was ready to respond, but no one asked for help. I was ready to be found, but no one was looking for me. I said, 'Here I am, here I am!' to a nation that did not call on my name."* The NIV says, *"I revealed myself to those who did not ask for me; I was found by those who did not seek me."* The NET Bible says, *"I appeared to those who did not look for me...did not invoke my name"* or even pray. The New Heart English Bible says, *"I have shown myself...I was near to those who did not seek me..."* God, contrary to popular views, is not hiding.

We Should be Seeking

Paul declared that God wants mankind to seek Him, even

if at times, it seems that we are groping in the darkness. Even at such moments, Paul asserted, *"God is not far from us"* (Acts 17:27). Quite the opposite. It would be, Paul said, impossible to *"live and move"* without Him. 1 Chronicles 16:11 advises us to *"Seek the LORD and His strength; Seek His face continually."* We are to set our heart and soul to seek Him (1 Chronicles 22:19).

God searches the Earth, looking for *"any who seek God"* (Psalm 14:2) and according to Jesus, for true worshippers (John 4:23). Proverbs 8:17 declares, *"those who diligently seek me will find me."* That requires searching *"for Him with all your heart and all your soul"* (Dt. 4:29-31). Jesus promised, *"seek, and you will find"* (Matthew 7:7-8).

WHAT NOT SEEKING SAYS ABOUT US

"The wicked," because of their pride, do not seek God. They are self-absorbed. They have concluded, *"There is no God"* (Psalm 10:4). Seeking itself is an indication of faith and a desire for righteousness. The end of those who do not want to seek God or know God, who refuse to give Him honor, is found in Romans 1:21-23: *"...they became futile in their speculations, and their foolish heart was darkened. Professing to be wise, they became fools."*

In the end, their discernment becomes so dull that they cannot distinguish between humanity and the animal kingdom, implying evolutionary atheism. Man, to them, is no more glorious than any other species. Paul says, what is *"evident within them,"* and by creation, *"evident to them"* (Romans 1:19), is suppressed. It is not that God cannot be known, but that man does not want to know Him. He does not like the revelation of truth from God that calls for repentance, that suggests that God is angry with ungodliness and unrighteousness (v. 18).

Thus, what can be clearly seen is obscured by a kind of self-imposed blindness. The darkness comes with the refusal to repent;

the resistance to worship, to honoring God. It is tied to the withholding of due thanks. The "futile speculations," the alternative worldviews, have turned the heart-lights off (v. 21). Having set forth a new way to consider creation, mankind professed themselves *"to be wise,"* and *"they became fools"* (v. 22).

TRUTH AVOIDANCE AND PRAYERLESSNESS

God can be known. Notice the phrases in Romans – *"evident within them,"* and *"evident to them"* (1:19). Here are the etchings of God on the walls of the conscience, the soul of man. Even in his fallen state, there is a witness that remains inside his soul. And there is also one in creation. Creation shouts, "There is a God; and the conscience echoes that truth." Man is without an excuse. *"Salvation is far from the wicked,"* and here is the reason: *"they do not seek Your statutes"* (Psalm 119:155). Here is truth avoidance, regarding God's moral law. Just as Adam hid, so mankind today hides and covers. He avoids God, and God's truth.

This is important to prayer – because truth avoidance destroys prayer. Suppression of truth turns the heart-lights off; it is a form of resisting God. Truth is like a light. With it comes revelation and insight. And by it, we are trued, changed, transformed (Eph. 5:8, 13; John 3:19-20).

PURSUING GOD

We noted earlier, in Genesis, that God pursued man. Of course, we are to pursue Him. God is looking for seekers; and seekers find God (John 4:23).

Hebrews 11:6 is one of the passages that tells us how we must come to God as we seek Him. *"Without faith,"* we are told, *"it is impossible to please God. He that comes to God must believe that He is, and that He is a rewarder of those that diligently seek Him."*

Seeking Him

The simple passage is stunning, packed with insights about the dance of faith and prayer. "Faith," the writer asserts, "pleases God" and makes prayer possible. But the goal of prayer in this passage is often missed. Prayer is not the pursuit of *things,* but the pursuit of God *Himself* – they that *"diligently seek Him."*

So much of our prayer is driven by personal needs. So little is driven by a desire for God, Himself, alone, above and apart from any other prayer outcome. This is prayer's real goal – *"to know Him, and the power of His resurrection"* (Phil. 3:10). We seek answers, breakthrough, commodities of various kinds, deliverance, effectiveness, the good life, finances, healing – and a ton of other things. Mostly we seek things from God's hand, not God, Himself. Psalm 27:8 instructs us, *"My heart says of you, 'Seek his face!' Your face, LORD, will I seek"* (See also: Hosea 5:15; Psalm 24:6; 105:4; 1 Chronicles 16:11; 2 Chron. 7:14). That's good advice. Perennially, the emphasis is on the 'face' of God.

> Prayer is the breath, the watchword, the comfort, the strength, the honor of a Christian.
> – Spurgeon

God – the Real Goal in Prayer

Faith is more than the acquisition of answers to our prayers. There are extraordinary outcomes to prayer. Propelled by encounters with God, common believers are thrust into positions of power and influence and they impact nations. History pivots. Such outcomes were rarely on the radar screen of these great people of faith. They happened as they pursued God, as they heard and obeyed him. If you ask these believers about the great joy of their lives, chances are, they will not brag about some gospel conquest, but about Christ himself.

Even noble prayer goals may be unanswered unless they are about accomplishing His will, glorifying His name, and advancing His kingdom (Mt. 6:9). Does God answer? Give breakthroughs? Send revival? Yes, and no. He is a rewarder of those who "diligently seek – *Him!*" God, Himself, is the great reward of prayer.

So prayer must seek to lay hold of 'the One who answers' instead of merely laying hold of 'an answer.' Seeking 'answers' and not 'the One who answers' is like leaving the well with a cup of water, when we could have had the well itself. Jacob was changed as he wrestled not with the promise, but with the One who promised.

Believing - Where We Put Our Faith

We have been taught the importance of faith, so we come to God in prayer, 'believing.' But the focus on faith in this passage challenges our conventional thinking.

First, we're told that we must believe that "He is," that God exists. Prayer is to be addressed to God, personally. It isn't talking to the walls or mere therapeutic sounds aimed at no one in particular. We must, to pray effectively, believe that "He is," that God is present as we pray, hearing our prayers.

Second, we are told that we must believe that He is a *"rewarder of those who diligently seek Him."* Faith in God's existence is explicitly required. Faith in his ability is implicitly required. We pray because we believe there is a God, and that He is able to answer. God hears (John 11:41-42); God answers. Most people pass the test of belief in God's existence and His ability to answer. It is the more 'precisely explicit focus of the writer of Hebrews that hangs us up in prayer – the need to believe that God is a "rewarder." This is faith in God's character.

We must believe, according to the text, that God is a good God, a benevolent, open-handed God, a "rewarder" – and that is where we experience difficulty. We declare faith in His existence and our confidence in His uncontested ability, but, we are not sure God will answer 'our' prayer, hear 'us' and grant us the petition we seek. We doubt His love for us – He must love others more. They, we conjecture, are holier, stronger, have more and better faith. So we seek out others to pray for us, confident that God will hear them when He won't hear us. Again, our problem is not a lack of faith in either His existence or ability. We wonder, however, is God so good, that His goodness would cause Him to answer me? Is His grace so deep, that He will respond to my prayer? Not being confident of His love, not certain that His love is rich and deep enough to love us – we disqualify ourselves, unaware that in doing so, we actually indict God. We fail to see the depth of His grace and forgiveness, how like an ocean is His love. We lack faith in His character.

Doubting God's Character – is Deadly

In Genesis 3, it was the character of God that the serpent attacked, *"Did God say...are you sure you can trust Him?"* Satan, through the serpent, indicted the character of God – and on that ground of doubt, Adam and Eve fell.

The complaint psalms are often deep laments over the personal confusion from some setback, some loss or defeat. When the psalmist had looked for God's victory and it did not come, he charged God with inaction, with not caring (Psalm 44:23).

The disciples did the same thing when they were caught in the storm, even with Jesus in the boat. He was sleeping – a parallel to the complaint psalms that accuse God of sleeping on the job. The disciples cried out, *"Do you not care that we are perishing?"* (Mark 4:38). Jesus rebuked them for their lack of faith – and here, we miss the point. The rebuke was not at their lack of faith in his ability; in fact, they were stunned, amazed, indeed, afraid of him, when he simply rebuked the wind and waves and brought calm. The rebuke for their lack of faith was not tied to Christ's ability, but to his character. His calm, sleeping state, in the midst of their storm, was interpreted by them as an absence of love. We do the same thing.

This is the great struggle of faith – to continue to believe in a good God in a bad and evil world; to continue believe that righteousness has a reward, and evil has consequences. To believe that Psalm 1, the prototype psalm in the Bible, with its clear crisp edges, is true – that righteousness has its reward; and evil, its consequences. To continue to believe when God does not answer.

Joining Prayer and Love

Paul suggests that the *"tribulation, or distress, or persecution, or famine, or nakedness, or peril, or sword"* (Romans 8:35) must not be interpreted wrongly by us. When such negative forces line up against us relentlessly, they sometimes cause us to mistakenly conclude, in despair, that *"we are being put to death all day long; We were considered as sheep to be slaughtered,"* sacrificed for some noble but unknown cause, expendable, and abandoned by God.

Paul argues quite the opposite: *"in all these things we overwhelmingly conquer through Him who loved us."* It is that certain sense of God's love that is the key to victory. In fact, neither *"death, nor life, nor angels, nor principalities, nor things present, nor things to come, nor powers, nor height, nor depth, nor any other created thing, will be able to separate us from the love of God, which is in Christ Jesus our Lord."*

This is our triumph, that we are centered in an unshakeable confidence in God's love – for us. If these 'things' can unsettle us, cause us to doubt God's love – the Evil One gets the upper hand. Victory is assured by our faith in His character.

Faith Works by Love

We don't have a faith problem, not precisely; we have a love problem. The goal of prayer – is intimacy with God. Not the acquisition of things, but the laying hold of God Himself. *"Faith,"* Paul declared, *"works by love"* (Gal. 5:6). If you are convinced God loves you – faith soars; and if you doubt God's love, it languishes.

We work on inflating faith – memorizing scripture, exercising our faith like we are lifting weights. Prayer and Scripture memorization are great exercises, but without a sense of God's love, you will always end up with a flat tire.

We enter prayer with a list of frantic 'God help me,' petitionary requests. We are sincere. We need God's help – He is there, and able. So we pray, passionately, fervently, sincerely, but all the while, we wonder – does God love me enough to answer this prayer? We may intercede for others with the same ambivalence. Here is a suggestion. Push back all the frantic and faithless 'God help me' prayers, as well as intercessory pleas for others. Push back the 'God use me, give me faith' prayers. We resist going forward in mission because we lack confidence in His watchful love and care.

Pray this simple prayer: "God, I know that you love me. And I love you with all my heart, all my soul, all my strength!" Pray it again, multiple times, with an emphasis on each word:

God – these are not just sounds, *this is prayer.*
I know that you love me. *No one must assure me.*
I *know* that you love me. *I know it.*
I know that you *love* me. *You love me.*
I know that you love *me*. *Me, yes, me.*

Don't stop – pray this a dozen times, a hundred times. This is not an exercise in narcissism. It is not meant to be a syrupy moment in self-indulgence. Nor can it be mere left-brain acknowledgement. "O, I understand that. I know that God loves me!" Stating it in such a cool, detached, non-emotional manner reveals the problem.

Love is catching, transferrable, virulent, transmittable. This has to be a heart-matter. When the understanding of God's love moves from our head to the heart – everything changes. With conviction, we say in response, "And I love you, Lord, with all my heart, and all my soul and all my might." We feel such love down to our toes. The love of God, like a flood, can't be contained by the levees of our hearts (Romans 5:5). It overflows. And it empowers faith.

Praying in Love's Embrace

God's love has a way of steadying us. It is not that we have laid hold of God, but God has laid hold of us – and when you feel yourself in His embrace, call it a shelter, a rock of defense, a fortress, whatever metaphor you choose, everything changes. God's love inspires confidence.

When we pray without a deep sense of God's love, faith is flat. And we end up asking God to do this or that, to prove that he loves us! Love must precede prayer. After Calvary, any arrangement that puts God in the position of having "to prove" His love is wrongful manipulation. In fact, faith soars when you know God loves you.

Praying that *demands* that God act to prove his love is an insult. God is no circus performer who should be asked to do prayer-tricks to prove his affection. The cross proved that. Now, having been given the greatest proof of love, *"He who did not spare his own Son, but gave him up for us all - how will he not also, along with him, graciously give us all things?"* (Romans 8:32), we pray with confidence.

The cross says, 'God will answer; God will respond with grace.' Notice Paul's language - *"how will he not?"* How could He do otherwise? It would be inconsistent with His character. He has, in Christ's crucifixion, invested far too much in us, not to hear our prayers. *"See what great love the Father has lavished on us, that we should be called children of God! And that is what we are!"* (1 John 3:1).

Jude, the brother of Jesus, giving prayer adviced, urged, *"keep yourselves in the love of God, expecting the mercy of our Lord Jesus Christ for eternal life"* (Jude 1:21). The ISV says, *"Remain in God's love,"* and the NET Bible, *"maintain yourselves in the love of God"* anticipating mercy.

The Greek word translated *keep, téreó,* means to *watch over,* to *guard.* It is a verb, denoting action, meaning, "I keep, guard, observe, watch over" whether or not I am centered, kept in and by, the love of God. It is the idea of being a prisoner of love, of staying centered, balanced, grounded in and by God's love. There is no healthy prayer life apart from God's love.

This is the manner in which we remain strong, *"...building yourselves up in your most holy faith and praying in the Holy Spirit,"* (Jude 1:20) and doing so in a way is that centered, anchored in God's love. Good prayer, enabled by the Spirit, strengthens holy faith, centering itself in an unshakeable confidence in His love.

Switching Motives for Prayer

Coming to God in faith, we have been taught, gains *answers* to prayer. God answers people who pray in faith. Yet, there is a dynamic in Biblical interpretation that seems, at times, contradictory. The truth is often like the sword, two-sided or double-edged. And in prayer, we often encounter this contradiction. For example, prayer does not seem to be primarily about answers. Nor does it seem to be about moving God to meet our needs. On examination, it seems to be more about God than us; more about His will, than our desires. It is not a transaction nearly as much as it is a context for transformation. God seems to be challenging our very motives for praying.

Praying for Answers

Praying in faith not only gains an audience, but secures answers – that we have all been taught. God answers people who pray in faith. *"Let us then approach the throne of grace with confidence, so that <u>we may receive</u> mercy and <u>find grace to help</u> us in our time of need"* (Hebrews 4:16 NIV).

God cares and answers us when we pray in faith. Hebrews 4:15 says, He somehow feels our pain. He is *"touched by the feeling of our infirmities."* Jesus himself promised, *"Whatever things you ask in prayer, believing, you will receive"* (Matthew 21:22).

God intends, indeed, He promises to answer us when we pray out of our relationship with Christ; *"If you abide in Me, and My words abide in you, you will ask what you desire, and it shall be done for you"* (John 15:7). A stunning promise.

Meeting Conditions

There are, however, conditions to our prayers - doubt forfeits answers. *"But let him ask in faith, with no doubting, for he who doubts is like a wave of the sea driven and tossed by the wind. For let not that man suppose that he will receive anything from the Lord"* (James 1:6-7). This instability goes back to not 'maintaining,' not 'keeping and guarding' our conviction, that God loves us. Instability comes when we doubt God's love. We maintain when we remain – in God's love. Everything falls apart in a relationship when love fails.

Praying Amiss

James points out another problem, perhaps the major problem, with unanswered prayer. *"You ask and do not receive, because you ask amiss, that you may spend it on your pleasures"* (James 4:3). Let's go back to Hebrews for a moment. *"Without faith,"* we are

> **Honesty and Grace**
> Retail store sign: "If you break it; you pay for it." Another store takes a different tack. Their sign reads, "Pick it up, look it over; if you break it, tell us, and we'll forgive you. Accidents happen." In the second store, the shoppers breathe easier. Grace prevails. Honor is a value and customers are not treated as liabilities. There is much more liberty and shopping, especially with children, is not fraught with anxiety. Each store operates out of a theological system – one out of law and works, the other out of grace. One encourages truth repression to avoid dishonor and a penalty; the other, candid but noble confession. In one, you pay for your sins; and in the other, you are forgiven if you are forthrightly honest. Both stores pay about the same amount for customer breakage. The second store is a lot more fun to shop in. Maturity, not perfection, is the goal; honesty is what God wants – just repent, which means, you say, "I'm sorry. I'm broken."

told, as we come to God – prayer – it is *"impossible to please him."* This is the other side of the sword of truth, the contradiction to common approaches to prayer.

What we have been taught is that in coming to God in faith, in moral purity, with clean hands – meeting the typical conditions outlined – we can expect God to answer. The difference here in Hebrews is subtle, but significant. Is prayer, wrapped in faith, the means by which we move God to answer? To please *us*, by granting *our* request?

Inverting Motives in Prayer

The Hebrews passage turns our prayer expectations upside down. Good prayer, wrapped in faith, is not the means by which we get God to please *us*; rather, good prayer is coming to the point at which the driving force of our lives is to please God.

We have made prayer about us, about God pleasing us, about God meeting our needs and answering us. It is clear, from the passages we cited, and others – God answers his people when they pray! He heals (Gen. 20:17). He delivers (Psalm 120:1). He sends rain (1 Kings 8:34; James 5:18). He intervenes in battles (1 Kings 8:44). He gives wisdom (Eph. 1:17). And more.

Here, in Hebrews, the great change comes in the transformation from getting God to please *us,* to our growing desire to please *Him* (John 8:29; 2 Corinthians 5:9; Colossians 1:9). The great acquisition, is not *things* – it is *God;* and the great transformation in prayer, is not that He pleases us, but that we live to please Him. Are you a God-pleaser or a self-pleaser? Or yet, a people-pleaser?

Jesus would hear the Father say, twice, *"This is My Beloved Son, with him I am well pleased"* (Mt. 3:17; 17:5; Mark 1:1; 9:7). The NLT says, *"This is my dearly loved Son, who brings me great joy."* Twice the voice boomed from heaven - at his baptism and on the Mount of Transfiguration. This should be the goal of every believer's life, to hear the heavenly affirmation, "I love you, child; I am proud of you." Make prayer about pleasing God!

Moving from Answers to Rewards

We relate prayer to answers; but in Hebrews, the pairing is between prayer and rewards. Jesus too, associates prayer with rewards (Mt. 6:6). Answers and rewards are not the same. Answers are at one level; and rewards are at another. God answers people who pray in faith. Dr. Herbert Lockyer, in his book, *All The Prayers of the Bible,* claims the Bible has 650 definite prayers, of which there are 450 specific answers recorded. But the real payoff in prayer is not answers. At times, we don't even know what or how to pray. At other times, we realize later, that God's 'No!' was a blessing. The real payoff in prayer is not answers – rather, it is rewards; not in our directing our lives from earth's perspective, but in God's provision of things we could not have foreseen as needs.

Rewards come, not from seeking the *hand* of God, but the *face* of God. As Hebrews 11:6 notes, *"He is rewarder of those that diligently seek <u>Him</u>,"* not merely something from Him, but Him. He is the great gift – and while he offers himself, we are too often satisfied with trinkets. Getting Him – we get everything we need.

Prayer is more than a divine requisitioning system. God also "rewards" us just for praying, that is, just for spending time before Him. In Mt. 6, Jesus promised a "reward" for praying. *"When you pray,"* he said, assuming that we would pray, enter your *"closet."* He expected us to maintain a secret place for prayer.

When we go to our secret place, God races there ahead of us. Sometimes He doesn't even disclose His presence. Jesus notes, He that "sees in secret" will "reward openly." God hides in our prayer closet and then manifest himself in the public square. The private moments of surrender translate into public God-moments punctuated with His Presence.

As we seek to please God, live in His love, refuse to doubt His character, wade through the pain of life with a certain resilience from above – God rewards us. And the rewards of praying are greater than the answers to prayer.

Establish a new benchmark for healthy prayer – "Father, I know that You love me, and I love You with all my heart, soul and might and I want to please You!" Meet God in prayer, when your only desire is to be with Him.

SECTION TWO
Personal and Family Prayer

CHAPTER 4
Personal Prayer – The Defining Mark of a Christian

Prayer is the defining, distinguishing mark of a true Christian.[1] Luther said, "He is no Christian who does not pray. As a shoemaker makes a shoe, and a tailor makes a coat, so ought a Christian to pray."[2]

"Man," Herbert Lockyer said, is "a praying animal." It is "the deepest instinct of the soul of man."[3]

It is impossible to find a truly great man of God who was not a great man of prayer. Bishop Asbury, renowned in Methodist circles, would rise at 4:00 a.m. and pray for two hours. Luther regularly spent the first two hours of the day in prayer.[4] Judson's work in China was aided by his midnight experiences. Henry Martyn, the English missionary, said there evolved a "strangeness" in his soul when he had spent too much time in public administration and too little time in private communion with God. Wilberforce called that "living far too public" and starving the soul.[5] Robert

Indicators of a Personal Relationship with Christ

1. <u>You talk with Him daily</u>. You pray. You live in His presence.
2. <u>You are conscious of His presence</u> and your conscious desire to please Him, to do His will (2 Corinthians 5:9; John 8:29). He rarely leaves your mind. You are preoccupied with Him. You are *"walking in the Spirit."*
3. <u>You are in love</u>! You are not merely doing religious things, keeping traditions, living by rules, honoring religious customs. No, you are in love! You know God is real. And you would do anything for Him.
4. <u>You delight in the Lord</u>, and therefore you embrace disciplines and duties that are not always delightful. You do so, out of love. *"If you love Me, keep My commandments!"* In the Old Testament, duty demanded that one keep the law. In the New Testament, love constrains us to do right. Our motivation has changed. Holiness, as the end result has not changed.
5. <u>You want to serve</u>. You are ready to be a bond-slave. Prayer makes us available. Prayer is the intentional and daily check-in experience. In prayer, we punch the divine clock and notify God that we are on-duty and ready to serve.
6. <u>There is an overflow of your life, outward to others</u>. The evidence of the inward love for God is read by others. They see it. You can't hide it. Prayer explodes outwardly in some manifestation of God's glory. His presence marks a life. This is "the glory!" How can you be silent? The love of God is shed abroad in your heart.
7. <u>The speech of an overflowing Christian is marked by thanksgiving and praise</u>. The inner flood spills out onto others around you. They are the benefactors of our satisfied hearts. The inner happiness becomes a river of joy tasted by others.

McCheyne vowed to not see *people* before he had met with God.

In many churches, prayer time brings a seemingly endless recital of needs, usually without any thanksgiving reports. The weekly episode becomes a silent faith crusher. Nothing is so small that it should not be taken to God in prayer. But petition is not the whole of prayer. And petition without a clear gaze at the One who answers prayer is unhinged praying. Prayer is not primarily a means of acquisition from God. In fact, the answers are the occasions by which we glorify God. Sadly, far too often, we are silent.

The heart of prayer is *communion* – oneness with God, unity, the celebration of our union, our peace with God through Jesus Christ. We can ask things only because we *"abide in Him"* (John 14:3). Without this vital relationship, there is no basis on which we can make requests. This connection allows us to intercede for others, especially those that have no relationship with Christ. And yet, it is simple communion that we most often fail to nurture in our prayer times.

Living in constant communion with God is the heart of prayer, and the essence of our faith. Everything rises and falls on the grace that flows through a healthy personal prayer life. Our time with God demonstrates our love, our longing for His presence, our willingness to be obedient. Through prayer, we present ourselves on God's altar.

Fifteen times the prayer life of Jesus is noted in the gospels – three in Matthew and four in Mark, Luke and John. "The Man Christ Jesus prayed; prayed much; needed to pray; loved to pray."[6] He began his ministry in prayer and ended it in prayer. He prayed in the morning (Mark 1:35) and into the night. He spent days in prayer (Luke 4:42; 5:15, 16; 9:18-31; Mark 6:30, 31). He prayed at his baptism (Luke 3:21-22) and on the Mount of Transfiguration (Luke 9:29; Psalm 34:5; 2 Corinthians 3:18). When he returned to the Father, it was to pray (John 14:16; 16:26; Hebrews 7:25). At the same time, He sent His disciples to a prayer meeting (Luke 24:14). His life was a life of prayer. Jesus came to the earth to pray. To be like Jesus means to pray.

MARKS OF AN EFFECTIVE PRAYER LIFE
1. Prayer and the Secret Place

A secret life of prayer is the key to successful public ministry. "The secret of praying is praying in secret," so believed Leonard Ravenhill. Jesus said, *"When you pray, go to your room...shut your door, pray"* (Matthew 6:6). Jonathan Edwards believed,

> If you live in the neglect of secret prayer, you show your good will to neglect all the worship of God. He that prays only when he prays with others would not pray at all were it not that the eyes of others are on him. He that will not pray where no one but God sees does not pray at all out of respect to God or with regard to His all-seeing eye.[7]

The practice of personal, at-home, daily prayer has reached an abysmal low. Prayer at church can't replace prayer at home. When Christians do pray during the week, they pray on the run. No quality relationship can be sustained with such a low investment of time and priority. Jesus assumed we would have a secret "place of prayer!" Luke captures Jesus praying *"at a certain place"* (Luke 11:1), indicating a favorite spot for prayer. Intimacy with God requires a "secret place of prayer!" It may be a closet or a corner, a room or a rocking chair. It may be a garden or a vista point. Such a place is sacred. Being in the place is a signal to God of our seeking, searching heart.

2. Prayer – The Secret to Spiritual Power

An encouraging trend is emerging. Serious Christians are creating prayer rooms in their homes. The rooms range in size from a large closet to a spare bedroom. Size is not nearly as important as the significance of the room. It should be a safe place to meet God and pour out one's heart.

Out of private meetings with God come public encounters with Him. Edwin Tull is fondly remembered as the Chaplain at

Lee University in the 1960's. He was raised on the Eastern shore of Maryland. When his mother's condition became untreatable, the family learned, "There is a preacher at the Church of God who believes God can heal." They called him. He came.

The praying preacher was not intimidated by the prognosis of the physician or the physical condition he encountered. He prayed. God came. And Mrs. Tull rose from her bed; that's also when Ed-

---

Suggested Items in a Personal Prayer Room

1. Maps of the world for mission praying. Particularly, maps which detail the nations yet to be reached with the gospel.
2. Missionary enterprises. Mission causes. Missionaries for whom you feel called to pray.
3. Maps of the US to pray for specific cities of America to see a revival and a great awakening.
4. Lists of national/state/county/city officials who need prayer!
5. A map of your city/county. Note the location of schools and even churches. Mark areas that are prone to high crime. Begin your own "spiritual mapping" project. Make the map a study of the city you live in and for which you have been called to intercede.
6. Family pictures as reminders to pray for children and grandchildren - and beyond them, for great-grandchildren.
7. Pictures or paintings that inspire prayer and intercession.
8. Prayer helps and guides.
9. Books on prayer, the devotional life, various translations of the Bible.
10. Carpet that invites prostration.
11. An altar for kneeling.
12. Space for prostration before God.
13. A chair for seasons of waiting.
14. Notepads to write and record insights.
15. The capacity to dim the lights.
16. The capacity for worshipful music, when desired.

win Tull fell to the floor in surrender. The moment changed his life forever. He met the God of the New Testament that day. His whole family was swept into vibrant faith.

What is the secret to such power? God shows up in public with those who meet him privately. Pastor C. J. (Pop) Abbott had a well-known habit of daily secret prayer by his bedside. Frequently and fervently he prayed there. Great prayer warriors have often knelt at their bedside so regularly, lingering there, that their knees wore grooves into wooden floors. Many developed prayer calluses on their knees.

3. Prayer – Moving from Duty to Delight

At the Tabernacle, days began and ended at the altar. The life of Jesus was marked by prayer that sometimes ran into the night. His habit was also to rise early to pray (Mark 1:35). David said, *"Early will I seek You"* (Psalm 63:1). Clyde Cranford urged, "Every morning, lean your arms on the window sill of heaven and gaze into the face of thy Lord."[8] Spurgeon said, "Prayer should be the key of the day and the lock of the night."[9]

Most of us think of prayer as *work!* Prayer is seen as a *duty,* not as a glorious privilege. Some Christians approach prayer as something necessary but undesirable. "I know that I *should* pray. That to grow in Christ I *have to* pray!" We lament, "If we are going to see revival, we must pray!" It is as if prayer is a kind of *spiritual castor oil* – not pleasant, but essential.

It is true, we *should* pray. We must pray. But healthy prayer moves beyond *duty* to *delight. Drawn* to God by love, not always *driven* by necessity, we long for His presence. Imagine someone saying to God, "In order to get this noble outcome, how much time do I *have* to spend with you? An hour? What would 15 minutes get? I want this blessing, this revival, *but I want it with as little time spent alone with You as possible!"*

Such a declaration is reprehensible, shocking, appalling. If we only want the *effect* of prayer, but not a deeper relationship with God Himself, we have revealed our true hearts.

Nine out of ten Americans pray. Seventy-eight percent pray at least once each week. Half pray several times a day. But the average prayer time is about five minutes.[10] These are fleeting prayers, prayers on the run, between business appointments. Delight makes *prayer itself* the main agenda. All other business is set aside. The day is spent with God! Daily prayer is an anchor. It resets our inner compass. It is a thermostat that regulates our temperament. By prayer, we tune our hearts to the music of heaven and ready ourselves to serve. We hear His voice and are more easily empowered to respond.

> **Prayer wonderfully clears the vision; steadies the nerves; defines duty; stiffens the purpose; sweetens and strengthens the spirit.**
> – S. D. Gordon

Few Christians have riveting spiritual encounters every day in prayer. God hides under our noses as we faithfully set ourselves aside unto Him. But our daily private discipline is inevitably linked to unpredictable and delightful encounters with God in the public square.

In contrast to our reticence, "The devil," Luther said, "is not lazy or careless, and our flesh is too ready and eager to sin and is disinclined to the spirit of prayer." The great reformer urged,

> Let prayer be the first business of the morning and the last at night. Guard yourself carefully against those false, deluding ideas which tell you, "Wait a little while. I will pray in an hour; first I must attend to this or that." Such thoughts get you away from prayer into other affairs which so hold your attention and involve you that nothing comes of prayer for that day...[11]

> **Prayer Treasure Hunt**
>
> Young people and young couples like adventure. I found a group of young adults who do "prayer treasure hunts." A treasure hunt is a popular yuppie event. You get a list of sometimes bizarre items and your team goes in search of the items. The first team to bring all of the items back to the site wins.
>
> The *prayer* treasure hunt is different. It isn't competitive; it's collaborative. The list is created by impressions out of prayer by the whole team.
>
> I was recently in a church in which they do prayer treasures hunts. Recently, after prayer and the recording of impressions, their list had such items as: "Target, Home Depot, Red Sweater, Nurse, Woman, Wife, Recent illness, Kitchen Utensil" and a few more items. Armed with their list, they headed first to the nearest Target store and began looking for someone with a red sweater. No luck. Then in the kitchen utensil area, they spotted her. They approached her and introduced themselves, then showed her their list. They asked, "Can you identify with any of these things?" She looked down the list. "Well," she said, "I am a woman, a wife, a nurse. My mother has been ill recently. My husband works at Home Depot." And then of course, she wanted to know, "What's this about?"
>
> They explained to her that she was "the treasure" that they felt God had sent them to find. They asked if they could pray for her – right on the spot. She wept.
>
> Does it always turn out like this? According to the group, "No!" But they have had enough treasure finds to keep encouraging them to get into the streets and "give the gift of prayer."

Francis Paget in the classic book *The Spirit of Discipline* described:

> ...the tremendous power of habit; the constant, silent growth with which it creeps and twines about the soul, until its branches clutch and grip like iron."

He warned that:

> ...the habitual drift, the natural tendency of our unclaimed thought, should be towards high and pure and gladdening

things." Discipline makes the difference – "the leisure time of life may either be a man's garden or his prison."[12]

The heart cry of every Christian should be for a daily rendezvous with Jesus. "I don't want the day to go by, without encountering Your presence in some significant way!" Adoniram Judson, the great missionary to Buddhist Burma prayed "seven times a day." Still he labored for six years without a convert. But 38 years later, he had recorded 210,000 conversions, one out of every 58 Burmese. Fruitfulness follows faithfulness. Luther said, "If I should neglect prayer but a single day, I should lose a great deal of the fire of faith."[13]

4. Prayer – Worshipful Love

We see prayer as one component in worship. It is one of many things in a worship service. At its heart and in its purest form, prayer itself is worship. And the heart of worship is our love of God. C. S. Lewis believed that "it is in the process of being worshiped that God communicates His presence to man."[14] The incomparable Christ is the treasure in the field, the pearl of great price, worth more than the world (Matthew 13:44-46). This discovery shifts our values, reorients and realigns our very life.

Such love demands passion. The maiden in the Song of Solomon says, *"Let him kiss me…his love is better than wine"* (Song of Solomon 1:2). The two lovers are on fire with desire for each other. The church at Ephesus was still standing, still working, still enduring, still upholding truth – but they had left their passion (Revelation 2:4). That drew a rebuke. It called for repentance. It predicted total backsliding.

Passion is essential in our relationship with God. William Cowper says that he had "known such exaltation that he thought he would die from excess of joy."[15] In the *Song of Solomon*, love is intoxicating. A simple kiss is disorienting, entrancing.

Our culture is passionate about everything but the right thing – sports, recreation, hobbies, money, automobiles, the adult toys we have come to afford, affluent lifestyles and more. Our passion belongs in two places – in our relationship with God and our love for our spouse (Ephesians 5:25).

We misplace passion. We think loving the Church is the same as loving God. It isn't. The Church is the bride and body of Christ, the object of his affection and his vehicle for service and witness. It is the visible expression of Christ in the Earth. We serve the Church, but our passion belongs to Jesus. The Church is not about itself; it is about Jesus. It is rightly constituted by members passionately in love with Christ, looking and living as if He might return today.

Worshipful devotion to the bridegroom can never be satisfied by *dutiful work*. Working for Him is not the same as worshipping Him. Worship at church cannot stand in the place of a daily, personal, at-home relationship with him. This does not diminish service in the church; it intensifies it. Because of this love, I work, witness and live in the blessed hope of his return. My work for Christ flows out of my worship. Spurgeon said,

> He who lives without prayer, he who lives with little prayer, he who seldom reads the Word, and he who seldom looks up to heaven for a fresh influence from on high – he will be the man whose heart will become dry and barren.[16]

5. Prayer – The Empowerment to Action

You've heard the expression, "There! I have said it!" Sometimes what follows is a good feeling; sometimes it is regret. Saying a thing empowers an idea in a way that merely thinking it does not. Saying a thing gives birth to a possibility. It pushes some inner thought to the outside. Others hear it, touch it, examine it, agree or disagree. It unifies. It polarizes.

We talk ourselves into doing things. Actions follow words. What we allow ourselves to say rises out of thoughts which we finally express. Something happens when we express these deep needs and longings, these hopes and dreams, these hurts and fears. Saying it is different than thinking it. "I am willing to go anywhere! Use me, God!" Or, "God, I don't want to do this!" Or, "God, I can't forgive him. I can't love her!" Such honest prayers reveal an inner resistance, but persistent praying changes us. "O, God help me love him. Help me forgive her. O, God – I want to please You!"

The Bible is a record of prayer – of praying men and women and what they accomplished. Praying believers have been change-agents whose mark on history seems timeless. Moved to act in faith, they accomplished things far beyond their own limited capabilities. The Scripture is a record of culture shifts affected by the energy from another world. Prayer moves us to action, and what is more important, it ties that personal action to the intervening action of God.

6. Prayer – As a Means of Filtering Toxic Thoughts

Prayer is a soul filter. Luther said the storms of life provide the opportunity for us to empty our cargo, "to speak with earnestness, to open the heart and pour out what lies at the bottom."[17] Alone with God in prayer, I am safe in pouring out my deepest feelings. Here, a therapy takes place. A cleansing comes. The Psalms give us blunt prayer language, full of despair and sometimes loaded with less than noble motives. But in the end, the psalmist turns his head upward and is reoriented. *"But, I will wait for You!"* (Psalm 59:1-10; See also: 71:14; 75:9; 77:10; 119:69, 78). In prayer, we pray through our own objections. We overcome our own noncompliance. We confront our own doubts. We face our own fears. We pray through such things and God gives us grace.

In the garden, Jesus said, *"My heart is nearly breaking."* The Greek word is *ekthambeo*. It means to be thrown into a state of fear or thoroughly amazed, to be astounded or struck with terror.[18] We can hardly imagine Jesus like this. *"Father, if it is possible, let this cup pass…"* (Matthew 26:39, 42). This is not something to be discussed openly with the disciples. He is with them, and yet removed. Only the Father can help him with this need. In prayer, Jesus moved to the place of total surrender. He prayed himself into complete alignment with the Father's will. He silenced any resistance in his flesh. Prayer summons the strength of heaven for the task (Luke 22:43). An Angel came to strengthen him. This is prayer.

> *And he left them again, and went away, and prayed a third time, saying again the same words* (Matthew 26:44). Paul would say, *"Concerning this thing I besought the Lord thrice, that it might depart from me"* (2 Corinthians 12:8).

Watchman Nee observes,

> The principle of praying thrice is to pray thoroughly, a praying through until we are clear on God's will, until we obtain His answer.[19]

7. Prayer Over An Open Bible

We allow an unhealthy practice when we consistently pray without a Bible. Good prayer is over an open Bible: *"Read the Word, and pray!"* The Bible is the Christian's prayer book. It is not to be read passively. It is to be read as if one were having a conversation with God. It is a love letter as well as an instruction manual for life. You read, and you respond in prayer. You borrow from the concepts and language of the Bible. You wrestle. You ask God, *"What does this mean? To me? Right now?"* In the pages of Scripture, we find the clearest and soundest resonance of God's voice. Walter Wangerin describes praying Scripture in this way:

> Imagine...the Psalm is like a house already built and that you are invited to enter there to make it your own. Praying from within the Psalm is to pray your own prayer...though you use words already written, you have become the present and living soul within those words.[20]

The Bible is to be prayed! You enter the Scripture and pray from within it. Luther said when he was cool or joyless, the condition was always traced to a deficit in prayer. Aware of the capacity of the "flesh and the devil" to "impede and obstruct" prayer, he developed a habitual response to coolness of heart.

> I take my little Psalter, hurry to my room, or,...where a congregation is assembled and, as time permits, I say quietly to myself and word-for-word the Ten Commandments, the Creed, and, if I have time, some words of Christ or Paul, or some Psalms, just as a child might do.[21]

"Prayer itself," Fosdick reminds us, "is a great conqueror of perverse moods."[22] Spurgeon wrote,

> We should pray when we are in a praying mood, for it would be sinful to neglect so fair an opportunity. We should pray when we are not in a praying mood because it would be dangerous to remain in so unhealthy a condition.[23]

8. Prayer As a Means of Purification

The old saying goes, "What's down in the well comes up in the bucket!"[24] Nothing will promote personal holiness as much as prayer and the study of the Word. The great Scottish pastor and writer Robert Murray McCheyne was asked what he felt that the greatest need of his congregation was "The holiness of their pastor," he responded.[25]

The church today is minimizing sin. We redefine sin as a "mistake." To be sure, any sin is a mistake, but it is more than merely stubbing our toe. Sin is deadly. It is toxic to relationships. It is a poison to the soul. Christians should never act as if the free blood of Jesus can casually be splashed about to cover just any sin. Such blood isn't cheap, even if grace is free.

Nathan said to David, *"The Lord has put away your sin; you shall not die"* (2 Samuel 12:13). Wow! David could have *died*. *"The wages of sin are death"* (Romans 6:23). Grace was never intended to foster the careless attitude toward sin that has emerged in the contemporary Church. Such a view not only misunderstands grace, it is a delusion (Romans 6:1-2). Sin kills. It is to be avoided at all costs. Grace is designed to not only deliver us from the curse of the law, but to deliver us to another law - the life-giving law of righteousness (Romans 6:18). Bunyan said,

> ...few of us can remember the last time we missed our bed for a night of waiting upon God for a world-shaking revival.
> - Leonard Ravenhill

> Prayer will make a man cease from sin or sin entice a man to cease from prayer ... Pray often, for prayer is a shield to the soul, a sacrifice to God, and a scourge for Satan.[26]

Over an open Bible in prayer, I find myself in need of change. Before the mirror of the Word, I see myself as falling short. Bunyan cried out, "O, the startling holes that the heart hath in the time of prayer!"[27] Repentance is the healthy reaction of an upright heart. Before God, we *"confess our sins and He is faithful and just to forgive us and cleanse us from all righteousness"* (1 John 1:9). Before one another, *"we confess our trespasses"* and He *"heals us"* (James 5:16). Clyde Cranford believed,

> We are never closer to God than in repentance. There, in humility and shame, we partake of the matchless grace of God, and the result is a deeper intimacy with Him and a greater sensitivity to His desires.[28]

William Carey noted, "Prayer – secret, fervent, believing

prayer – lies at the root of all personal godliness."²⁹ The capacity to engage with a holy God and not change is a tribute to the insidious nature and strength of sin's hold within us. Face-to-face with a holy God, the great prophet Isaiah cried out, "*I am undone, a man of unclean lips*" (Isaiah 6:5). And so must we. Crooked hearts dodge repentance and remain deluded; those that are tender break before God. Richard Foster notes,

> To pray is to change. Prayer is the central avenue God uses to transform us. If we are unwilling to change, we will abandon prayer as a noticeable characteristic of our lives. The closer we come to the heartbeat of God the more we see our need and the more we desire to be conformed to Christ.³⁰

Prayer deals with the toxins that collect in the soul. It purifies. In prayer, I take my anger and cynicism, my unbelief and despair, my disappointment and fear of failure to God. There, in the presence of a holy and loving Father, I find myself saying, "*But, God I really want to be like you. I want to be free of this. I want you to change me, strengthen my faith and cause me to triumph.*"

If we would go to God in prayer with all of our deadly and carnal inclinations and not to our neighbor, talk to no one about our hurts and disappointments until we talk to God, it would cure a great deal of gossip and slander in the church. Prayer corrects wrong thinking. It realigns character. It nudges us toward Christlikeness. Richard Foster adds, "*When we pray, God slowly and graciously reveals to us our evasive actions and sets us free from them.*"³¹

9. Living In An Atmosphere of Prayer

We are to "*pray without ceasing*" (1 Thessalonians 5:16). If prayer were talking, how could we do that? If it was primarily comprised of religious activities, how would that be possible? No! Prayer, at its deepest and purest level, is living in unbroken fellowship with God. Out of this communion, we offer our needs to God, and He enters into our lives with His bountiful supply. Out of this connection, we intercede for others. In a state of peace, we engage in the warfare of prayer, confident of our victory. As Oswald Chambers observes, "Prayer is not an exercise. It is the life of the saint."

Relationships need unhurried time. Our relationship with God is no exception. God's design was that once a week, an entire day was to be set aside to walk and talk with Him. The rhythm of our lives should make time for God. The feast days, Israel's holidays, were holy days, days to be spent advancing their relationship with Yahweh. God was on the calendar of his people Israel – daily, weekly, monthly (the new moon), and seasonally (festivals and holy days). Is He on your calendar?[32] R. A. Torrey declared:

> When the devil sees a man or woman who really believes in prayer, who knows how to pray, and who really does pray, and, above all, when he sees a whole church on its face before God in prayer, "he trembles" as much as he ever did, for he knows that his day in that church or community is at an end.[34]

10. Prayer as Transformational

In our world, faith is increasingly marginalized. "Newton banished God from nature, Darwin banished Him from life, and Freud banished Him from His last stronghold, the soul."[35] Christ is seen as an additive to enrich our lives. Biblical principles are viewed as informative for a more productive life. Man supposedly has a small tear in his soul and the cross is a repair kit. Such notions are radically inferior to the true New Testament perspective.

Christianity is not a sweet supplement. Christ did not come to make men better. He came to make men new. The theologian Emil Brunner said *"Only he who understands that sin is inexplicable, knows what it is!"*[36] It is *"the mystery of iniquity"* (2 Thessalonians

Ten Ways to Deepen Your Communion with God[33]

1. **Sit quietly.** Enjoy the very real sense of His presence. Let Him lead. Don't rush the moment. Let his peace renew your soul.
2. **Listen.** Listen deeply. Tune your soul to His stillness. Listen to the rumblings of your own soul, and let God quiet your inner storms. Be still before Him. "God speaks in the silence of the heart. Listening is the beginning of prayer." – Mother Teresa
3. **Yield** to God's action. Let Him come near. Let Him move around you, encircling you. Put yourself in a "Here am I!" position.
4. **Let God speak.** Avoid the temptation to break a holy silence. He may speak through scripture, through a life-experience, through the memory of some history you share with Him. Listen for any word the Spirit might bring.
5. **Keep a prayer journal.** Record your impressions and thoughts. Note scripture references. Write down promises you make to God and those you sense him making to you. Make notes of action items – things you are led to do; and change points – things you are led to change.
6. The essence of the prayer relationship is love. **Let God love you.** And then, express your love to Him. Let Him lead with love. Let Him love first.
7. **Take a walk.** Drop everything. Go and get alone with God. Or, take a drive. No agenda. No list. Just a spontaneous encounter with God.
8. Then go to your **secret place.** Get your journal. Write. Record the fresh insights. Pour your soul out. Tell God your deepest needs. Share your secret thoughts. Praise God - verbally. Confirm your love. Offer needs.
9. Sometimes you may find yourself at a parallel to some moment in Scripture. What is happening to you has happened to David or Paul, or some other Biblical character. **Let the Bible give you language** that expresses the depth of these encounters with God. The Psalms are especially helpful in cultivating our prayer vocabulary. Athanasius, the fourth-century Egyptian theologian said, "Scripture speaks to us; the Psalms speak for us."
10. Sing. Shout joyfully. Dance. **Celebrate his presence.** Glorify him. Give voice to the deep sense of his presence. Be spontaneous. Be grateful to and for a God who pursues you. Weep. Weep deeply over the wonderful grace of his embrace. Tears have a way of cleansing the soul. Weep joyfully. Weep over the wonder of why he loves you so.

2:7). Human acts are sometimes bizarre and unthinkably wicked. Yet our culture rationalizes away a personal devil that tempts and twists the nature of men. We are getting help with evil! (Ephesians

2:2). And we must get help to do good. Salvation is a liberation event, wrestling us from the powers of darkness. It is the transfer from the body of Adam to the body of Christ (Jude 1:23; Romans 5:12-21; 1 Corinthians 15:45-49). It makes all things new.

Saved and now liberated, man is free to worship, free to do right, free to serve God. And this freedom must be exercised. So many Christians define themselves in terms of what they *don't do* or where they no longer go. But a man or woman is not free if he is only *"free from."* We must be *"free to"* – free to pray and praise, free to worship and witness, free to bless others and demonstrate love. Freedom *from* is neutrality. It is only in the embrace and exercise of our new liberty, specifically in the area of the disciplines of faith, that we move forward and stay free (Romans 6:13, 16, 18-22). The discipline of prayer is at the heart of this new liberty.

In a lifestyle of dependence, I am led by the Spirit, directed and renewed. In humble dependence, my confidence in God grows. I hear His voice. I obey. I am being transformed. G. Campbell Morgan said, "The prayer life consists of life that is always upward and onward and Godward."[37] Leonard Ravenhill charged, "Today God is bypassing men – not because they are too ignorant, but because they are too self-sufficient. Brethren, our abilities are our handicaps, and our talents are our stumbling blocks!"[38]

1. "Prayer," *Zondervan's Bible Dictionary* (Zondervan's Pictoral Bible Dictionary: Grand Rapids, Mi; 1963), 678. (Quoting Friedrich Heiler: *Prayer*. New York: Oxford University Press, 1932, 119.)
2. Quoted in John Gray, *The Biblical Museum*, v. 5 (London: Elliott Stock, 1878), 127.
3. Herbert Lockyer, *All the Prayers of the Bible* (Grand Rapids, MI: Zondervan, 1959), 17-18, see also 192.
4. E.M. Bounds, *The Power of Prayer* (Christian Art Gifts, Inc., 2007) 46.
5. Ibid, 99.
6. Lockyer, 181.
7. Jonathan Edwards, *The Works of President Edwards* (Worcester: Thomas, 1809), 219.
8. Clyde Cranford, *Because We Love Him: Embracing a Life of Holiness* (Multnomah Publishing: Sisters, OR; 2002), 109.
9. Charles H. Spurgeon, *The Treasury of David* (Hendrickson Publishers, 1990).
10. George Barna, *The Index of Leading Spiritual Indicators*, 61.
11. Martin Luther, "Luther's Way to Pray," *The Contemporaries Meet The Classics on Prayer*, ed. Leonard Allen (West Monroe, LA: Howard Publishing, 2003), 72-73.
12. Francis Paget, *The Spirit of Discipline* (London: Longmans, Green and Company, 1893), 71.
13. Lockyer, 133.
14. William Thrasher, *A Journey to Victorious Praying* (Moody Publishers, 2003), 203.
15. Harry Emerson Fosdick, "The Problem of Moods," *The Contemporaries Meet The Classics on Prayer*, ed. Leonard Allen (West Monroe, LA: Howard Publishing, 2003), 160.
16. C.H. Spurgeon, *Day by Day with C.H. Spurgeon* (Kregel Publications, 1992), 83.
17. Martin Luther, "The Psalms As Prayer," *The Contemporaries Meet The Classics on Prayer*, ed. Leonard Allen (West Monroe, LA: Howard Publishing, 2003), 40.
18. <www.studylight.org/lex/grk/view.cgi?number=1568>. Also see: *Strong's Exhaustive Concordance*: 1568 and 1569.
19. Wathman Need, *Let Us Pray* (Christian Fellowship Publishers, 2009).
20. Walter Wangerin, Jr. "The Psalm as a House," *The Contemporaries Meet The Classics on Prayer*, ed. Leonard Allen (West Monroe, LA: Howard Publishing, 2003), 42.
21. Martin Luther, "Luther's Way to Pray," 72.
22. Fosdick, 162.
23. Ibid, 163.
24. Cranford, 36.
25. Robert Murray McCheyne, *From the Preacher's Heart* (Scotland: Christian Focus Publications, 1995), 14.
26. <thinkexist.com/quotation/prayer_will_make_a_man_cease_from_sin-

or_sin_will/188755.html>.
27. Ibid, 160.
28. Cranford, 40.
29. Richard Foster, "The Main Business of Life," *The Contemporaries Meet The Classics on Prayer*, ed. Leonard Allen (West Monroe, LA: Howard Publishing, 2003), 16.
30. Ibid.
31. Ibid, 17.
32. See *The Praying Church Resource Guide* for a sample schedule for a Personal Prayer Retreat and a Couple's Prayer Retreat. P. Douglas Small, *The Praying Church Resource Guide* (Kannapolis, NC: Alive Publications, 2013).
33. Eugene Peterson, "Praying by the Book," T*he Contemporaries Meet The Classics on Prayer*, ed. Leonard Allen (West Monroe, LA: Howard Publishing, 2003), 53.
34. R.A. Torrey. <www.gotothebible.com/HTML/Sermons/powerofprayer.html>.
35. Gerald Heard, Quoted by James S. Stewart, *A Faith to Proclaim* (New York: Charles Scribner's Sons, 1953), 76-77.
36. Ron Phillips, *Vanquishing the Enemy* (Cleveland, TN: Pathway Press, 1997), 29.
37. <www.liftupusa.com/pquotes.htm>.
38. Leonard Ravenhill, *Why Revival Tarries* (Bloomington, MN: Bethany, 1959, 1987), 39.

CHAPTER 5
The Process of Personal Prayer

Prayer is simple and childlike. And yet there is an order about prayer.

First, Pray Always

Pray *"on all occasions!"* (Eph. 6:18; 1 Thess. 5:17; Luke 18:1). Prayer should be sprinkled into every aspect of our lives. It should be natural and spontaneous. By praying, we invite God into our lives. So, pray – as you drive to work, as you sit in your home, as you look at the beauty of nature and hear the birds sing. Pray – when you entertain friends and as your children come and go. Prayer must never be foreign to daily life. It is not to be a strange exercise offered once a week in a building with colored windows.

We are to pray everywhere (1 Tim. 2:8), about everything, and in doing so, we involve God in our lives. There is never a time when prayer is inappropriate. There is never a mood in which prayer is not fitting.

- Pray – when you are depressed (Psalm 42).
- Pray – when you are happy (Psalm 9:2).
- Pray – when you are angry (Psalm 4:4).

- Pray – when you are tempted (Matthew 4).
- Pray – when you are weak and feeling alone (Luke 22).
- Pray – when your faith seems to be failing you.

And when you pray, be real with God (Matthew 26:41). Authentic natural praying is best. We noted earlier that a time and place of prayer is critical. Thus, we pray at a specific place and that empowers prayer every place. And we prayer at a regular time, and that encourages prayer all the time. Those who have no set place and time of prayer are less likely to be inclined to pray all the time, everywhere.

Second, Pray According to the Word

The Bible is our prayer book. From it we draw the language to pray. On the basis of its promises we argue our claims in the courtroom of heaven. By it, we are guided to make corrections in our own lives, change our plea, deepen our intensity or discover some answer we had not seen before. From its pages, God speaks most clearly. Scripture comes alive. New meanings emerge. Our hearts are strangely warmed. Our minds understand. Our spirit is renewed. Pray over an open Bible. Pray consistently with Scripture.

Third, Pray With the Enabling of the Holy Spirit

The Holy Spirit acts as a counselor in prayer. He aids our praying (Jude 20; Matthew 20:22; John 4:10; Romans 8:26-27). So, you may pray *"in the Spirit!"* You should always pray *"with the Spirit."* Prayer in the Spirit moves us from misguided, to Spirit-directed praying. It prevents our *"praying amiss"* (James 4:3). The Spirit *"helps our infirmities: for we know not what we should pray...but the Spirit himself makes intercession...for the saints according to the will of God"* (Romans 8:26-27).

Prayer by the enabling of the Spirit moves us from not knowing, uncertainty, to a certain knowing. This is not something the head knows, but something about which the heart is certain. God has heard. He has answered. The matter is settled. But prayer needs balance. We pray by the unction of the Spirit, but also *"with understanding."* We speak and pray mysteries, but prayer should also enlighten us. The mind is to be edified as well as the spirit.

> Calvin Miller agrees, "When the knee bends, character is born." A kneeling body without a bent heart means nothing in the throne-room of heaven, but a humble heart along with a bent knee "is an indication of how we see the Almighty."[1] It is humility exemplified. "When the knees bend, the King comes!"[2]

Prayer informs. It reveals. It uncovers hidden things and places them before us as logical and explicable concepts.

Better praying isn't found by "trying harder" but by "yielding sooner." The quickening Spirit brings passion, but he also knows how to help us pray.

Fourth, Pray in the Name of Jesus
(John 14:13; 15:16)

A majority of Americans believe that "all people pray to the same god...no matter what name they use for that spiritual being."[3] The name of Jesus is not a magic word Christians say at the end of a prayer. Its power is far beyond that. With the enthronement of Christ the spiritual economy of the world changed. Christ became the High Priest in heaven's tabernacle (Hebrews 8:1-3). He desires to connect every human to his Creator-Father by his priestly ministry (Exodus 19:6; 1 Peter 2:5). The invocation of his name in our priestly ministry provides the opportunity for him to reveal himself as alive to an unbelieving world. Jesus said, *"Until now you have asked nothing in My name. Ask, and you will receive"* (John 16:24).

♦ We pray in his name because through him we have direct

access to the Father.
- ♦ We pray in his name to honor his sacrifice at Calvary.
- ♦ We pray in his name because he came to us from God and now invites us to use his name when we approach Yahweh as Father.
- ♦ We pray in his name because he died and rose from the dead – he is alive.
- ♦ We pray in his name because we are promised spiritual treasures in his name.
- ♦ We pray in his name, because we, his bride, have taken his name and we are championing his cause in the earth.
- ♦ We pray in his name, because our new identity is fused with him – we are members of his body.
- ♦ We pray in his name in a desire to make our requests consistent with his life purpose, with what he came to do and with how he lived.

We pray in his name because no one has ever walked on the earth comparable to him – fully God and fully man; love and truth fused together – not compassion without principle, nor yet principle without love. He is no mere man. No one is in his class. He is incomparable, exalted, above and apart from all other humanity and all gods. *"There is no other name given among men whereby we must be saved!"* (Acts 4:12) God has given him a name above every name! (Ephesians 1:21; Philippians 2:9)

> Public prayers are of little worth unless they are founded on or followed up by private praying.
> – E. M. Bounds

He commanded that we pray in his name, not merely as a memorial to him but because of the consolidated power represented by his name. Six times in John's gospel the command is repeated – *"in my name"* (John 14:13-14; 15:16; 16:23, 24, 26). Jesus is not just one more way to heaven (John 14:6; Acts 4:12). If the Father sacrificed his only begotten son to create one more way among many, he is not a beloved Father to be trusted and adored. Such a father would not be a good father. There is only one way to God, and that is through Jesus, the Christ, and it is because there was no other option for redemption than the direct intervention of God, in Christ, that he came.

To deny prayer in the name of Jesus alters the Christian faith. It is an attack on the heart of that faith. How can there be Christianity without the Christ? It is more than another ethical system. Christians have a relationship with the indestructible Christ. Out of the vitality of that relationship we live. Jesus is more than a good model. He is more than a mere inspiration. He is more than a great teacher. He is God and Savior, our Kingly Lord! To deny him is to deny our faith. To be told that we cannot pray "in the name of Jesus" is the very spirit of antichrist.

Fifth, Pray that God Be Glorified

"*Whatever you ask in my name, that will I do, that the Father may be glorified!*" (John 14:13) When our purpose is to glorify the Father, Jesus will bring all the resources of heaven to bear on our request. "Every answer to prayer," Andrew Murray says, has "this [the glory of the Father] as its object: when there is no prospect of this object being obtained. He will not answer."[4] God's glory is the end of prayer. It is why Jesus came, "*I seek the honor of Him that sent Me!*" (John 5:44)

"*Father, glorify your Son, that your Son may glorify You.*" (John 17:3). Glory comes to those who give glory to God. In a culture where self-interests are the strongest motives behind prayer,[5] the answers will be meager! We are "praying amiss!" To *do all* to the glory of God requires that we *ask all* for the glory of God. "These twin commands are inseparable: obedience to the former is the secret of grace for the latter."[6] Richard Foster argues,

To ask "rightly" involves transformed passions. In prayer, real prayer, we begin to think God's thoughts after Him: to desire the things He desires, to love the things He loves, to will the things He wills. Progressively, we are taught to see things from His point of view."[7]

Jesus was consumed with giving the Father glory. He has been crowned with glory. If we order our lives to give Christ glory, he will crown us with glory.

Sixth, Pray to the Judge of the Universe, the Father

Technically, our prayers are addressed to the Father. We also pray to and through Jesus, our attorney-priest who represents us. We pray by the enabling of the Holy Spirit who helps us. Prayer, at times, is a formal legal petition presented in heaven's courtroom. Only citizens of heaven have access there. Only those whose names are in the Book of Life gain admission. Only those in a covenant relationship through Jesus Christ may appeal to the benefits in the covenant. In heaven's courtroom, those who present their claims must pray based on Scripture, consistent with God's holy nature and according to His will.

The only way you and I have a claim on heaven's throne is by our relationship to Christ and our position as bride-partner and believer in the new covenant by His blood. We have no other basis for appeal. All court systems operate on the rule of law! So does the court of heaven. Christ did not come to destroy the law of God, but to affirm it and answer it by grace (Matthew 5:17; Romans 6). It is our covenant standing that gives us the privilege of prayer, of accessing the throne of God. In prayer, we file our petitions, and place a claim on the storehouses of heaven based on the finished work of Christ.

Seventh, Pray Submitting to the Will of God

In prayer, we bow! We kneel. We bend our stiff hearts. We humble ourselves. We come with a contrite and broken spirit. Prayer alters our attitude. It invites dependence, rather than independence. It engenders confidence, not in the flesh, but in the Spirit. Without prayer, we remain a proud and self-sufficient people always at arm's lengths from God because, *"God resists the proud, but He gives grace to the humble"* (1 John 5:14-15; James 4:2-3).

Prayer inverts our passions. We pant, not for the world's satisfactions, but for the water-brooks. We hunger for God. Such Spirit primacy in a fleshly culture is rare. So many prayer efforts today are attempts to get God to agree with us. Real prayer brings us into agreement with him. Insights come. Sensitivity to the Spirit is heightened. We are readied to be His instruments. *"Not my will, but Your will be done."*

Eighth, Pray with Eternal Kingdom Purposes in View

In prayer, we invite God's reign. We plead for the "will of God" to be done in our lives and His holy name glorified. We invite heaven to invade the earth. We pray and worship with eternal outcomes in view. And that necessitates the investment of more than mere time – it demands the application of heart. Finney would say, "There can be no revival when Mr. Amen and Mr. Wet-Eyes are not found in the audience." Especially when 'amen' is understood as a verbal and prayerful affirmation of what is being prayed or preached. It is to say not only a passive 'yes, I agree' but a 'yes, so be it' and that with the intention of agreeing to the point of action. Wet-eyes is the sign that the heart is praying, as well as the head.

Summary

So, we pray always. We live in a spirit of prayer. We pray according to the Word of God, prayers informed by Scripture. We pray by the enabling of the Holy Spirit asking for an anointing to pray. We pray in the name of Jesus. We pray to the Father, the Judge of the universe. We pray, submitting our requests to the will of God. We pray with Kingdom purposes in mind, not merely with a view to our own self-interests. The Scripture teaches us that "God could be approached *anywhere* but not *anyhow* (John 4:24)."[8]

Conclusion

Prayer is the defining factor in the war with the flesh. The *"spirit is willing, but the flesh is weak."* The presence or absence of prayer is often the simple difference between our defeat or victory. The athlete who believes he can win on chance or talent alone without the regimen of training necessary to succeed is deluded. He may win a few amateur contests, but he will not progress far beyond that without the disciplines that sharpen the edge of mere talent. It is the exercise of godly habits, including prayer, that allows us to confidently enter the contests with the flesh and the devil as fit instruments for God. At one level, God protects our innocence – and as a David, we slay our Goliath. But then, God requires us to practice the rigors of warfare without which we will surely fail.

Flabby Christians who consistently ask grace to do what righteous disciplines should do in response to grace will rarely be catalysts for a significant move of God. The absence of the discipline of prayer will manifest in fleshly ways, aberrations that eventually eclipse our Christ-likeness. Conversely, the presence of the healthy discipline of prayer is one of the indicators that we will win the war

> **Involving Your Body in Prayer**
> "If we do not involve our bodies," Martin Smith argues, " ...we may not be able to enter a true, attentive stillness because our posture frustrates it ..." The result is often a drowsy condition punctuated with "pins and needles and restlessness. More than that," Smith adds, "We remain inhibited in our self-expression... If in prayer we shut down all bodily gesture and movement and confine ourselves to a single position we cut in half our power to feel and own and express our devotion, our love and our needs..."[9] Jews rock back and forth in prayer. Pentecostal Christians in the early years were physically expressive in prayer. They lay prostrate. They stood. They paced back and forth. They lifted hands. They bowed heads. They shouted and wept. They doubled over as if feeling the burden about which they were praying. Their faces were tear stained, anguished. The hands were at times open. Their fists were at other times tight, with white knuckles, as if they were engaged in a fight. Their whole body prayed.[10]

with the flesh and the devil – for in prayer, we access greater grace in which we are able to stand. Not falling into sin is so often traceable to the quiet time with God that started our day.

Grace is not merely the reach of God that compensates for our failures. Grace is the evident power of God that works in us at the moment of the test and allows us to overcome. Grace is the invisible hand that keeps us after we have sinned. Prayer produces saints – men and women whose lives are marked by godly character, who have been graciously enabled to live beyond the grip of sin. Grace and the grit of discipline go hand-in-hand.

"Consider!" Paul instructs us (Colossians 3:5-10; Romans 6:11). Challenge the way to see things. A new mindset is required for the effective Christian. But the change cannot be merely rational. *"Now...put them all aside"* – and he names the works of the flesh which must be abandoned and left by the side of the road if we are to continue on salvation's journey. But then, still more is required. The *"putting off"* is followed by the *"putting on"* (Colossians

3:9). And the "putting on" alters our thinking even more – *"put on the new self who is being renewed to a true knowledge according to the image of the One who created him"* (Colossians 3:9-10; Romans 6:6). Habitual sin is the sign of an undisciplined mind. The discipline of prayer forces us to breathe the fresh, clean air of heaven that purifies the mind.[11] Francis Paget says, "Your thoughts are making you. We are two men...what is seen and what is not seen. But the unseen is the maker of the other."[12]

---

1 George Barna, *The Index of Leading Spiritual Indicators*, 23.
2 Andrew Murray, "The Chief End of Prayer," *The Contemporaries Meet The Classics on Prayer*, ed. Leonard Allen (West Monroe, LA: Howard Publishing, 2003) 11.
3 Ibid, 12.
4 Ibid, 13.
5 Richard Foster, "The Main Business of Life," *The Contemporaries Meet The Classics on Prayer*, ed. Leonard Allen (West Monroe, LA: Howard Publishing, 2003), 11.
6 Calvin Miller, "When the Knee Bends," *The Contemporaries Meet The Classics on Prayer*, ed. Leonard Allen (West Monroe, LA: Howard Publishing, 2003), 138-139.
7 Ibid, 143.
8 Herbert Lockyer, *All the Prayers of the Bible* (Grand Rapids, MI: Zonservan, 1959), 78.
9 Calvin Miller, "When the Knee Bends," *The Contemporaries Meet The Classics on Prayer*, ed. Leonard Allen (West Monroe, LA: Howard Publishing, 2003), 139.
10 Henri Nouwen, "Resistance to Prayer," *The Contemporaries Meet The Classics on Prayer*, ed. Leonard Allen (West Monroe, LA: Howard Publishing, 2003) 139.
11 Clyde Cranford, *Because We Love Him: Embracing a Life of Holiness* (Multnomah Publishing: Sisters, OR; 2002), 159.
12 Francis Paget, *The Spirit of Discipline* (London: Longmans, Green and Company, 1893), 73.

CHAPTER 6
Family and Faith

An American preacher recently conducted a Bible literacy test on Sunday morning. The results were staggering. In a congregation that numbered 300, many could not identify *Calvary* as the place of Jesus' death. *Gethsemane* rang no bell for 43 percent. *Pentecost* had no significance for 75 percent. Only five percent got a score in the range of 90-100. Only 12 percent answered 70 percent of the questions correctly. About 80 percent knew fewer than half of the answers to simple Bible facts. Does it make a difference?

A prison survey of 1,700 inmates found one man from a home with a history of a daily, old-fashioned, family altar. This man was later found innocent and released! One thing was common among the 1,699 other men found guilty of crimes worthy of incarceration – no family altar.

Fifty years ago, multiple voices – the church, the home, the school, neighbors and friends, the business community, government and more – reinforced the same values. The voices still sound forth, but not congruently. They espouse different values, but their voices are increasingly resonating together with decidedly anti-biblical values. The number of books used in the public education of our children, if placed in a stack, would reach a height of about 17 feet high, equivalent to two-stories. But in that pile of books there would be no Bible. And at those schools, there would be no officially sanctioned Christian prayer.

Increasingly, conservative students and their Christian faith are being persecuted. Christian ideas censored. Christian subjects disapproved for papers. But as significant and perilous as this trend appears, the problem cannot be fixed by merely returning prayer and Bible reading to schools.

Families in this nation stopped praying at home long before the privilege of praying in schools was taken away. We've made a great deal about the removal of prayer and Bible reading in school. But the greatest loss is the absence of prayer in the home. Lockyer declares, "True family life is dependent upon family recognition of God."[1] That recognition can't be incidental. It must be intentional.

Faith In the Home

The Bible says in Deuteronomy 6:1-7,

These are the commandments...the Lord God commanded to teach you, that you might do them...That you might fear the Lord your God, to keep all His statutes and his commandments, which I command you, and your son, and your son's son, all the days of your life; that your days may be prolonged...that it may be well with you, and that you may increase mightily, as the Lord God of your fathers has promised you, in the land that flows with milk and honey.

You shall love the Lord your God with all your heart, with all your soul, and with all your might. And these words, which I command you today shall be in your heart; you shall teach them diligently to your children, and shall talk of them when you sit in your house, when you walk by the way, when you lie down, and when you rise up.

Faith is transmitted inter-generationally, from father to son. The place of transmission and training is not the synagogue or

> ### Bless Your Children
>
> Ultimately, every father is a priest and prophet to his family. No man has a right to die until he has blessed his children. The act establishes the notion of spiritual legacy. The act positions the father in place of being the spiritual leader he should be, and it calls sons to the position of being a man of God in their home. The power of blessing, of imparting grace, of inviting God's hand that traces the generations, is not a mere symbolic thing. Something very real happens in such moments. Isaac longed to bless his son. Esau had no appreciation for the blessing. He was a fornicator, which may not be a reference to sexual sin, but something deeper. Esau could only see the present pulsating moment. He is the exemplary existentialist. Jacob, though fraught with character flaws, seemed to recognize that there was something in the blessing that was larger than his life-span, something bigger than himself, something that would live beyond his father's time and pass not only to him but through him to the generations. The blessing invited Jacob into a timeless status, not merely by receiving it from his father Isaac, but by his position as a link in the generational chain through which the blessing moves on.
>
> Every father should bless his children. Lay hands on them. Pray over them. Pass on a blessing. Do it early in their lives. A common practice now is to begin to pray for children while still in the womb. Read Scripture to them, pray for them, bless them. Continue to pray for them when they are adults and you are in the autumn years. Bless your children and your grandchildren. Make a formal ceremony of it. Seal it with some symbolic act or gift. Make it unforgettable.
>
> I have begun to ask God for special grace on ten, no twenty, generations if Jesus tarries. Will You bless my children's children's children? Guide. Keep them. May they walk in Your ways and know You deeply. May they do something great for the Kingdom! May they accomplish things I could never have accomplished.

the temple, or by inference the church. It is the home. The home has always been the institution upon which God depended for the transmission of faith.

While "sitting in the house" or "walking by the way," when

"rising up" in the morning or "retiring in the evening," there were conversations about the Lord. Spontaneous faith lessons were to occur. Praise was heard. Sincere prayers were to be prayed. Every day, God was acknowledged. He was never taken for granted, never ignored. Silence does not honor Him appropriately.

In the Christian home, as it was in the Hebrew home, it should be a normal thing for children to hear parents talk about faith. The atmosphere of the home should be filled with audible and visible signs of our love for God. These were not to be formal teaching sessions held four times daily. This was incidental teaching. It was teaching that was as natural as breathing.

Parents who love the Lord openly create an infectious environment in which their kids catch the faith. Intentional teaching and training are essential. But incidental inculcation of values is even more powerful. If how we live and spontaneously respond to the challenges of life does not reflect deeply held practices, all our intentional efforts will fall flat.

Formal prayer and worship times are important. But it is the flavor of the home that is so radically transforming. It is the diligent love of the Lord, not merely dutiful devotional times. It is having "the words" in our hearts that naturally springs to conversations with and about the Lord while sitting in the house and talking. It isn't what we try to do – it is what we most naturally do! It is the natural bubbling up of our love for the Lord that spills out on every aspect of family life and does so in a way that is natural and not contrived. When we get up, we praise Him. When we walk by the way and notice a sunset, we offer gratitude. When we lie down, we whisper worshipful thanks. When we sit by a child with a fevered brow, we sing prayerfully to the Lord.

> The truths that I know best I have learned on my knees. I never know a thing well, till it is burned into my heart by prayer.
> – John Bunyan

The Scriptures instructed the wearing *"on the hand"* and *"between the eyes,"* actually on the forehead, the symbols of faith. The very placement of these symbols is suggestive. Faith was to affect doing (the Scriptures were to guide the hands) and our seeing (we understand things by the lens of Scripture; our worldview is out of Scripture). *"On the posts"* of the house and *"on the gates"* were also visible symbols of faith (v. 9). Both the people, along with their children, and the places where they lived were to be marked as belonging to God. Such deep spiritual deposits never get away from a child.

Couples Praying Together

Every husband and wife should pray together, daily if possible, not less than weekly.

- A cup of coffee in the morning combined with a morning prayer is a simple and good way to begin the day.
- Add a devotional.
- Read Scripture together.
- Read through the Bible together in a year.
- Select a Christian book to study together.
- Pray together regularly for your children and grandchildren. Call them by name. Pause over each name.
- Give the Holy Spirit an opportunity to impress your heart and mind with others in view. That could lead to some adventuresome days.

The Christian Difference

In 2004, George Barna released a report that found no difference in the divorce rate among Christians and non-Christians. Additional research indicates that there is more to that story. For couples who attend church regularly, the divorce rate drops by 35 percent. That's significant.

A University of Chicago survey revealed that 75 percent of the Americans who pray with their spouses reported marriages that were "very happy." Those who prayed together were more likely to respect each other, discuss their marriage goals together and, in a surprising find for the University, report high levels of satisfaction in the area of couple intimacy.

New data indicates that when a couple has received pre-marital counseling, and they not only attend church regularly, but take faith home and pray together, the probability of divorce is one in 39,000. Church attendance is good – a modest drop in divorce. But praying together pulverizes divorce. This is the power of faith, and of practicing faith together.[2]

The Prayer Difference

Tom and Liz were in trouble. "It was very dark. There was no love there. Alcohol had come in," Liz said. Tom added, "I think it was bringing the Lord into our lives" that changed our marriage. The couple says that praying together saved their marriage.[3]

Doug and Beth also had a marriage that was strained. Three children, two job changes and two 1,000-mile moves had stressed the relationship to the breaking point. Beth, in a bold attempt to save the relationship asked her husband Doug to begin praying with her. Doug was not a Christian. In fact, he was a nonreligious, self-proclaimed man of science. But he felt that if saying prayers with Beth could save the relationship, it was worth a try. His discovery was revealing: "I soon found that praying together brings out a real sense of selflessness and humility," Doug noted. "When you're praying for each other, and not yourself, you're focused together and speaking from the heart on a whole different level. I would never have predicted this for us, but it really works."

"As bad as any problem may seem at that moment," agrees Beth, "prayer always helps us see beyond it. It doesn't have to be a long, drawn-out Scripture reading, just a few minutes a day. When we pray, it brings another level of honesty to our conversations. I think it's the most intimate thing you can do with another person." Now they pray together every night.

Julie's marriage was also strengthened as a result of prayer. "It's pretty short and not at all scripted," she says about the giving of thanks before each meal. "We just join hands and let it rip. Whether we're asking for forgiveness or giving thanks, saying it out loud holds a lot of power. Most marriages require a ton of faith," Julie declared. "You've got to believe that somehow the two of you are going to make it through things. You've got to believe that you're being blessed with this person."

Prayer Implications for a Couple

When a couple prays together, they create a safe and regular forum to process daily issues before God. They invite God into personal and marital struggles. Each hears the concerns of the other, especially spiritual and relational burdens. They develop a capacity for greater openness with one another. The bond between them becomes stronger – not just physical attraction, but a more holistic bonding takes place involving the emotional and spiritual levels. Their unity increases. They find themselves consistently on the same page about issues they face. They invite God to intervene in their lives and the lives of their children. And He does.

Couples who pray about their family, business concerns, their finances, their giving to the kingdom, their involvement in God's work report miraculous results as a fruit of prayer. The number of disagreements declines. Couples are taking their stresses to God in prayer, looking to Him for answers. As a result, they tend to be more patient with each other, see things from an eternal perspective. They lay a spiritual foundation for a spiritual legacy for their children.[4]

Prayer Goals for a Couple

Beyond praying for one another, and the needs of family and the home, a couple might do the following:

- Pray daily for your children.
- Pray for unsaved family members and friends, work associates and neighbors.
- Designate at least one day a week or month to pray for your pastor and other spiritual leaders.
- Pray regularly for some ministry of the church.
- Adopt at least one missionary for prayer. If you can't send financial support, pray for them – daily, if possible. Keep up with them. Pray into their needs.
- Adopt a nation, and jointly intercede for a great awakening in that nation. Trace developments there. Pray for missionaries there. Let God use you to change a nation.
- Adopt an unreached people group. Make it your prayer project. Pray until you have heard that God has raised up a missionary to go and reach them, then pray for that missionary.
- Adopt a para-church ministry for prayer – one that works with the local schools, the homeless, unwed mothers, seniors, prayer and unity causes in the community.
- Pray for political leaders – choose one: a mayor, a city-councilperson, a state legislator or senator, a congressman or senator, the President or a member of his staff. Send them a note – "I am praying for you."
- Create a couples' prayer triad with two other couples and adopt mutual projects for prayer. Confer with one another

Couples Prayer

Five minutes in the morning and again in the evening can save a marriage. When a couple prays together, the rate of divorce is one couple in 1,150.

Suggestions for connecting through prayer:

- In the morning, smile. Say, "I love you!" Kiss. Embrace for a full minute. And pray. Invite God into the embrace. Pray a prayer of blessing one for another. If nothing else, repeat the Lord's prayer together. Read a passage over one another out of the Psalms.
- In the evening, when you first connect again after a working day, repeat the process.
- Read the book, *Moments Together for Couples,* a great devotional to use to enrich the marriage.
- Once a year, do a spiritual retreat together. As a part of that overnight, consider an inventory of your relationship. Using passages like 1 Corinthians 13, 1 Peter 3, Ephesians 5, and even Romans 12-13, read the passages and note areas in your own lives where you need improvement. Make a list. Then exchange lists. Pray and ask God for grace to change.
- Pray for your children.
- Set marriage goals, spiritual and financial.
- Encourage personal growth in God.
- Turn off the TV and spend time talking. Talk and then pray. Pray and then talk. Learn to move effortlessly between dialogue with one another and prayer to God. That makes God a party to your conversation. Don't ignore Him. He's in the room.
- Have communion together. Wash one another's feet.
- Expand your daily times to fuller devotional encounters. Do it three times a week as a minimum. Pick out a book to use as a joint study. Grow together.

monthly. Share information about the people, the ministries, the causes about which you are praying. Pray for one another's kids. Get together once a quarter for an evening of prayer and sharing.

Don't merely use prayer to your personal advantage. Pray for others, particularly for the kingdom purposes of God. Be missional in your praying. Pray with harvest eyes.

Church at Home

In one season of our life, we held a weekly "home church" experience. Our children led the informal event. They chose the worship choruses. They sang the special songs. They gave testimonies of thanks to God for some experience in their lives. They prayed prayers. They read Scripture. They performed skits and little dramatic vignettes. They practiced for these moments. At times we had a bit of bickering in the middle of the worship event but what church doesn't. Occasionally, we had to pause and put them back on track. I wish this had been longer than a short season. It was priceless. Probably, life-changing. The best worship is close to home, daily, allowing for encounters with God.

The book *Grandma, I Need Your Prayers* contains this wonderful story:

> I learned the Lord's prayer, at the age of five, sitting on a stool at my grandmother's knee...When she tucked me in bed, she would thank God for the day with a long prayer. In the morning, she'd ask me to say, 'Amen!' to that prayer and she'd start the day, praising the Lord. Whatever came up during the day, she'd stop and talk to the Lord about it carrying on a conversation with Him as though He was right there in the room...She made God as real as the man next door...She loved me so unconditionally.[5]

The New Testament instruction for transmitting faith is found in Ephesians 6:4, *"And, you fathers, do not provoke your children to wrath, but bring them up in the training and admonition of the Lord."* This command is specifically for fathers. A Swiss study indicated that when a mother attended church without a father, the likelihood of the children attending church as adults dropped drastically. But when a father attended church, even without the mother, the number of kids inclined to attend church as adults stayed the same, and in some cases increased. The power of a father's example in faith is profound.[6]

It is fathers, specifically, who are urged not *"to provoke their children to wrath."* They were not to relate in a way which irritated or exasperated a child. They were to avoid provoking negative behavior. Relationships were to be framed in ways that invited a positive response. This means that a father must know the temperament and personality of each child.

The second command is positive. Fathers were to bring their children up in the *"nurture and admonition"* of the Lord. Our children are our first disciples! They go everywhere with us. They learn to talk like us, gesture like us, duplicate our habits. They even look like us.

> Some people pray just to pray and some people pray to know God.
> - Andrew Murray

The home is God's discipling institution and children are the disciples of Christian parents! The first tool in the discipleship arsenal is nurture. It involves love, positive correction, instruction and when necessary redirection. *Admonition* means warning and reproof. It is the Greek word *"nouthesia,"* from *"nous"* meaning "mind" or "intellect," and *"tithemi"* meaning "to put or to place." It is the idea of "putting or placing something in the mind." It implies content. The father helps the child see positive alternatives to life choices. Admonition is not the same as prohibition. It doesn't simply say, "No!" It points out the right way!

In the American society, we accept the responsibility for the care, basic provision and shelter of our children, but we have allowed the State to assume responsibility for the education of our children. And we have asked the church to assume the responsibility for the moral education of our children. This was never the intent of God. It is not what the Bible teaches.

Let the Children Pray!

Children long to pray. They are natural pray-ers! Tom Bisset in his book, *Why Christian Kids Leave the Faith* found that something had happened that had not allowed them to explore inconsistencies that troubled them. They did not see faith working in "real life" ways. So they never personally owned the faith! They had conformed to standards to avoid parental confrontation, but they had never been deeply transformed.[7]

Still, Bisset says,

> God is everywhere...always seeking His own. Walking away from your faith is not simply a matter of washing your hands of God...He is ceaselessly calling His own back to the Father's house. It does not matter that these wanderers refuse to listen...will not attend church or that they become silent when the conversation turns to spiritual things...if they refuse to read the Bible or pray...they cannot escape from the God who is everywhere and who is always speaking.[8]

A grandmother with two three-year-old granddaughters said,

> I get up early in the morning to pray and read the Bible... when the grandchildren wake up and come out of their bedroom, I'm in my chair praying. They snuggle up with me as I finish. I'll read a few verses or pray aloud...they learn this is the normal way I start my day.[9]

Dale Evans was 35 when she came back to Christ. She learned Christian principles at the feet of her grandmother. One of her ancestors had been jailed for street-preaching instead of adhering to the Church of England. Incarceration couldn't stop him. He preached through his jail cell window to people below. "His genes are strong in me!" Dale said, "His heritage is partly the responsible for my forthright declaration of Christian faith in the midst of a show business career, even at the expense of a contract."[10]

1. Herbert Lockyer, *All the Prayers of the Bible* (Grand Rapids, MI: Zonservan, 1959), 20.
2. See also *The Praying Church Resource Guide,* Section 3.
3. "Couples That Pray Together – A report by Heather Sells," CBN News, March 23, 2008.
4. Adapted from *Your Wife Can Be Your Best Friend* by Clarence Shuler. Used by permission of Moody Press, Chicago, IL, 1-800-678-6928.
5. Quin Sherrer and Ruthanne Garlock. *Grandma, I Need Your Prayers* (Grand Rapids, MI: Zondervan, 2002), 28-29.
6. Robbie Lowe, "How Father's Faith is Crucial to Children's Faith" <www.ad2000.com.au/articles/2003/oct2003p10_1457.html>.
7. Tom Bisset, *Why Christian Kids Leave the Faith* (Grand Rapids, MI: Discovery House Publishers, 1997), 157-158.
8. Ibid, 205-207.
9. Quin Sherrer and Ruthanne Garlock, 43.
10. Dale Evans with Carole C. Carlson, *Our Values* (Grand Rapids, MI: Revell, 1997), 86.

CHAPTER 7
The Family Altar

In Genesis 12:7, *"The Lord appeared to Abram and said, 'To your descendants I will give this land. So he built an altar to the Lord, who had appeared to him'"* (NASB). The altar here, built by Abraham, was a family altar. It was to solidify the promise of generational provision. That is what a family altar does – it preserves the promises of God now and in the next generation. The promises of God cannot and must not stand alone. They demand our response. And prayer, the essence of the altar, is our response. Prayer grasps the promises. Prayer says, "Yes and amen!"

Through the centuries, family worship was the norm for Christians. In *Nead's Theological Works*, an 1850 publication, we find, "Heads of families ought to observe prayers with their families, mornings and evenings. This is generally termed 'Family Worship.'"[1]

Through the centuries, Christians have gathered twice a day for corporate prayer: morning and evening. This pattern goes back to the morning and evening sacrifice in the Old Testament tabernacle. Morning prayer begins the day; it tunes hearts to heaven. Evening prayer closes the day, committing it to God, allowing for confession of any sense of failure and conversely, the celebration of

Praying With and For Your Kids

1. **Praise God for His creation. Pray spontaneous prayers of praise when nature's beauty is so apparent.** Point out rainbows and the colors of the fall, springtime flowers with the buzzing bees and the singing birds. Thank God for such a beautiful earth.

2. **Point out answers to prayer and celebrate them with your children.** Encourage them to share God's answers to their prayers. When you entertain ministers and missionaries or praying Christians, have them share answers to prayer. Stories are the means by which we pass on God's active work in history.

3. **Bless your children.** When your child is hurting, turn the situation into prayer time. They will never forget the association of pain and prayer. When you are wounded or in despair – PRAY! It is a life lesson. Bless them. Invite God into their difficulty. Lay gentle parental hands of love on them. Pronounce a Biblical Blessing over them. Read a passage of scripture to them, out of their Bible. Mark it so they will remember it as a promise from the Lord.

The Daily Blessing. Invoke Numbers 6:24-26 over your children.
"The LORD bless you and keep you; the LORD make His face shine upon you and be gracious to you; the LORD turn His face toward you and give you peace."

---

4. **Teach your children about the armor of God.** Help them understand that life is a battle. But, we all have been given critical tools that assure us victory (Ephesians 6:10-18).

5. **Establish a family worship time.** Create a time when the whole family commits to be together. Worship. Sing. Read Scripture. Do that systematically (through the Psalms, or the Gospels, or a Bible Story Book). Share needs and pray for one another. Take some principle and talk about its meaning. Do this at least once a week.

6. **Lace prayer into family gatherings.** Don't just give a birthday gift and light candles. Pray for the birthday child. Bless them. Ask God to guide their lives and help them make a difference in the world. Say, "We thank God for _____, a gift You gave to us. What a wonderful boy/girl s/he is – a treasure to us, and a gift to the world." Have them pray a prayer, "God, thank you for the gift of life ... Help me live my life to honor you ..."

7. **Pray for people in need – on the spot.** Ask God to bless at an accident scene. Pray for the homeless you see on the street. When exposed to a problem on the television news – pray, then and there. Spontaneously. Teach your children to pray about everything. Prayer invites a compassionate heart. It keeps us tender. It reminds us that we should care. Life without prayer creates spiritual and psychological barriers to life, that sees tragedies unfold and does nothing. It promotes a lack of empathy, a disconnect.

8. **Make Holidays Holy Days.** Read the Christmas story at Christmas and take time to thank God for the greatest gift of all – the Christ child. Consider a family gift to God, and His work at Christmas. At Thanksgiving, pray prayers of thanksgiving!

9. **Prayer-walk your neighborhood.** Take a family walk and pray all along the way. Bless the families that live in your neighborhood. Teach your children casual and informal prayer – under the open heaven, as they walk along. Get the video, *Prayerwalking for Kids,* from Joey and Fawn Parish.

10. **Pray for city and national leaders.** The National Day of Prayer Task Force wants families to adopt a local, state, or national political leader. In doing so, the family commits to pray for and communicate with this leader for at least one year. Find resources at: www.nationaldayofprayer.org. There is also a wonderful video that teaches children about the 10/40 Window called The 10/40 Window for Kids available on youtube.

11. **Take your family to prayer events.** When the church has a prayer meeting, take your children. When National Day of Prayer gatherings take place on the 1st Thursday of May, take your children. Other similar community prayer events include PrayUSA!, Praying Through the Window, March for Jesus, the Global Day of Prayer, Meet Me At the Pole, September 11 Prayer Gatherings at the Courthouse, Meet Me At City Hall. Encourage your children to take part in such prayer events.

12. **Keep a family prayer journal.** Record family answers to prayer. Significant spiritual experiences. Promises of God. Make a place for each child. Journal the spiritual experiences, even the struggles and the prayers you pray. What a gift that will make some day. Keep records of missionaries the family has committed to pray for. Make the connection between prayer and people coming to know God. Pray for neighbors. Pray for enemies. Let your kids hear you bless them.

some God-moment in the day. It allows us to enter the rest of God as we retire.

One hundred and fifty years ago, family worship was common. Christian families prayed together, daily. Home altars and worship centers were common. Guests participated. Worship consisted of Bible reading, prayer and singing. The family altar declared dependence on the invisible guest of the home – God Himself. It said, "We are not alone!" On special occasions, prayer was offered. In good times and bad, seasons of transition and triumph, the family gathered to pray. Whenever something good happened, they would stop and offer prayerful thanks. When danger threatened, they prayed. Family prayer times don't have to be long, Ten to fifteen minutes may be sufficient. Consistency is more important than length.

Changing Times

Abraham was a sojourner, but he took his faith and his altar with him wherever he traveled. His tent might have been pitched on different turf, but his altar anchored him to the same God. "Abraham was a man of the altar." Matthew Henry said, "Where ever he had a tent, God had an altar…sanctified by prayer. He erected his own altar that he might not participate with idolaters in the worship offered upon theirs."[2] The family altar differentiates us from the pagan world around us. It identifies our children with the precepts and presence of God. It is a compass and an anchor.

In pre-modern times, the hearth where the food was prepared was the focus of the home. From it, the family was fed. At it, the family was kept warm. Out of it, light shone into the darkness. Around it, in the evening after supper, the family gathered for prayer. The fireplace was a reflection of the ancient altar which was always associated with fire.

> **Family Altar Dedication**
>
> From colonial days to the late 1800's, almost every devout Christian family in America had a family altar. Practically every day, the family had prayer together. Without a television or modern entertainment center in the home, the family found interest in faith and one another. After dinner, the family Bible was opened and typically the father read to his family. Each family member prayed. Songs were offered. The experience anchored the family to faith, and to God. It did not have to be a long experience. In those days, the fireplace was often the area around which the family gathered.
>
> The Hindu often has a sacred space in his home. The Buddhist may have such a place as well. What would happen if each Christian family dedicated a space in their home for a sacred assembly? It may not be used exclusively for prayer. But it should be arranged for that use. It may mean the installation of a cross or a special picture, a shelf with faith symbols that provide some visual focus – a banner or a table centerpiece. Have each member of the family bring items to create the family altar space. Here the whole family will meet with God. Here memories will be made that are marked by family encounters with God. Here prayers will be offered and recorded. Here, answers to prayer will be announced and celebrated.
>
> When a family altar is established, it should be dedicated and anointed as a sacred space. Introduce the idea of the family altar. Have a workshop. Offer models for family worship. Have small groups actually experience the models, as if they were a family. Provide resources. After the launch of family altars, have a follow-up meeting. Have couples share the good and bad stories. Encourage them to persevere.

In the 20th century, family worship began to experience a marked decline. Christian education took place in the Sunday School. Prayer and worship occurred at church. As the industrial revolution intensified and fathers left the home for work in factories, a strange view of men emerged in America. Men were increasingly considered worldly, women were pure. Men were breadwinners in the vile world; women kept the hearth in the virtuous home. Men traded their roles as spiritual leaders in the home for role as providers outside the home. Today, the home is often little more than a place where we sleep and keep our stuff. Many families do not share meals together. Such practices do not create healthy families that model biblical purpose.

The greatest need for prayer in the Christian community is in the Christian home. The disappearance of the family altar has come simultaneously with the breakdown of the family and the culture war on our youth. Geroge Barna says we are only churching three percent of "Generation X." We are losing our own kids to the world. The absence of prayer in the home is more damaging than its absence in the church. In fact, when prayer is something strange and foreign to daily life, we have created something very different from New Testament Christianity.

Renewing the Practice of the Family Altar

In a survey involving 1,000 churches, parishioners were asked, "Why does the church exist?" Eighty-nine percent responded, "To take care of my family's and my needs."[3] It's the wrong answer. The church is not about us. It is about God. We have everything upside down in our me-first culture. The church cannot care for personal and family spiritual needs in a one-hour, once-a-week experience.

Without the family altar, Christianity is in danger of becoming a "just-for-Sunday" activity. The family altar marks the home. It invites conversation about the God we serve. It centers us daily. It defines who we are – a family belonging to and representing God. It differentiates us from world around us. Many of our homes have nothing that sets them apart from the non-practicing Christians next door, except a few religious items. The family altar is a reminder that, "We are the people of God!" Prayer at and around it creates unforgettable expressions that anchor us for a lifetime.

Some traditions publish books to use as prayer guides. You may choose a less formal approach. What is important is to develop some plan – systematic readings, regular prayer focus points,

Christian development issues. Also remember, prayer was never intended to be a monologue. God talks to us, too. Teach your children to hear from God through Scripture and through the Holy Spirit's gifts.

A Physical Space

Everything needs a place. Different rooms in our houses are designed for different uses. Everyone and everything need space – a place to fix broken things, to cook and sew, to laugh and sleep, private and public space, personal and shared space. The Christian family needs a place to meet with God – the family altar. Some traditions encourage their families to construct an altar in their homes for family worship.

The place does not have to be fancy. It should be noticeable enough to provide focus. It should be marked as special. At the altar the family will experience their most vital activity – prayer, reading Scriptures and family worship. Every family altar should be unique to the family, but certain features will be common.

Some altars are designed like the tabernacle, to face the rising sun. This is a symbolic daily reminder of the coming of Christ, the Sun of Justice (see Malachi 4:2). Some altars have above them a wall-mounted shelf and under that a small table or dresser covered with a decorative tablecloth. On the shelf or the table is a cross, candles, an open Bible, prayer aids, anointing oil.

Family worship should never be a dread or a burden, strained or awkward. It should be a natural part of family life. The appointment with God should involve the whole family. When guests are present, keep your appointment and invite their participation. What a witness that can provide. If your children have friends over, tell their parents, "This is the evening we have family worship! Would you mind if your child joins in?"

> **House Dedication**
>
> When you move into a new house, call a group of Christian friends over to pray though the house. Dedicate it. Pray in every room. Pray in the yard. Anoint the house with oil. Read Scripture in it and over it. Ask God to make this a house of peace in the neighborhood. Pray, "God, if any evil has transpired here, forgive and purify. If any evil spirit has found a home here or has been invited here by any former resident, we declare this a house dedicated to the living God and made holy by his presence. No evil is welcome here." The goal is not to become mystical. Such moments are extremely practical. They set up boundaries and expectations for you and your family. Pray: "May we be witnesses in this neighborhood! May we live in a way that glorifies You! May we welcome into this home friends and strangers, and may all note the difference that Your presence makes. Be Lord of this house!" End your house dedication with the renewed dedication of your family, *"As for me and my house, we will serve the Lord"* (Josh. 24:15).

Our Jewish Prayer Heritage
The Family in Prayer

The Jewish pattern is still a sabbath family faith experience every week. Every conservative Jew, in his youth, knew where his family would be on Friday evening. By sundown, the preparations would be made, the table adorned and the candles lit. Prayers would then be offered and songs sung. There would be recitations for the children. Repetitive acts. Theology was laced into the ritual along with a dash of mystery. The litany was rich with variety. Each family member had a role. The weekly repetition marked the home as belonging to God and each member of the home as being a part of the covenant family. Through 1,900 years without a homeland, a holocaust and countless experiences of repatriation, these people survived and tenaciously held to their identity.

The regular experience of seeing Dad and Mom pray, of singing and praying together as a family, marks Jewish children to this day with a distinctive identity. They never get away from their roots. These weekly faith and prayer ceremonies anchor them as a people. Even non-practicing Jews recognize their Jewishness.

Perhaps our aversion to ritual has inoculated us from such practices. Or it may have been the years in which the church steered away from Jewish roots and substituted Christianized pagan holidays. Whatever the reason, there would be value in recovering home-based faith celebrations which express the Biblical calendar.

The Feast Days – Faith Celebrations

The Old Testament feast days contained the gospel message in code. They were not merely cultural festivals; they were prayer events. Combining a party with prayer is a tough concept for us. Of course, the feasts also contained solemn moments. The altar was a busy place on such occasions. There, the nation met with God. What are the feasts and their themes all about? What are the encoded messages?

- ◆ *The Passover* – Pointed to Christ the Lamb, the Redeemer.
- ◆ *The Feast of Unleavened Bread* – Pointed to the need to purify the homes and be set apart as the people of God, freshly redeemed, separated from the world as Israel was separated from Egypt.
- ◆ *The Feast of the First Fruits* – The first sheaf of the spring harvest was raised in the temple and offered to God as a promise of the coming harvest. The dead seeds, buried in the ground, had come to life. So, Christ is the first fruit of the resurrection from the dead. His life promises life to us. His resurrection is prophetic of our resurrection.
- ◆ *The Feast of Pentecost* – Looked to the giving of the Law and the coming of the Holy Spirit. In the New Testament,

the Spirit writes the law on our hearts and guides us into truth.

- *The Feast of Trumpets* – Looks forward to the return of Christ.
- *The Day of Atonement* – Looks to the Great Day of the Lord.
- *The Feast of Tabernacles* – Looks to the reign of God in the earth.

This panoramic scope of the gospel message is the eschatological calendar of God's work in a time-space world. What would it look like for a family to use this annual calendar to reinforce God's redemptive story? To teach and pray around each theme. To have special family festivals and celebrations. Each feast has a theme:

- *Passover* – Redemption. Salvation. The blood of Christ, the Lamb. Protection. Deliverance.
- *UnLeavened Bread* – Purity of life and home. Sin's (leaven) effect. Separation from the world. Leaving our Egypt.
- *First Fruits* – Christ, our hope of resurrection. Being raised in Christ. Eternal life. Dying to self, living in newness of life. New beginnings. Promise and hope.
- *Pentecost* – The coming of the Holy Spirit. Spirit-fullness. The inner life of God. Truth in our inward parts.
- *Feast of Trumpets* – Looking for the return of Christ. Living with an eye toward the eastern sky. The blessed hope. Last Day events.
- *Atonement* – Christ the atonement. Gratitude for sins forgiven. Teaching on the consequences of sin. Recognizing the coming Day of Judgment. Distinguishing the Judgment Seat of Christ from the Great White Throne Judgment.
- *Feast of Tabernacles* – Camping with God. Looking forward to the Reign of Christ. Knowing there is a life beyond this life. Living with eternity in view. Teaching our kids that we are a pilgrim people, just passing through this world.

> **Keep A Family Prayer Journal**
>
> Howard Hendricks, a Professor at Dallas Theological Seminary, says his wife kept a journal of the family's prayer experiences. She wrote on one side "We asked!" And on the other "He answered!" It was a priceless reminder to their children and grandchildren of how God worked and is still working in their family tree. The Old Testament is a kind of prayer journal for the family of Abraham. It traces God's faithfulness to his children through the centuries.
>
> Record family answers to prayer and significant spiritual experiences. Note the promises of God to the family. Make a place for each child. Journal spiritual experiences, even the struggles and the prayers you pray. What a gift that will make some day. Keep records of missionaries the family has committed to pray for. Make the connection between prayer and people coming to know God. Pray for neighbors. Pray for enemies. Let your kids hear you bless them.

A Family Faith Calendar

Add to these Christmas and Resurrection Sunday (which often coincides with Passover and the Spring Feasts). Using such an annual calendar every year would provide the opportunity for parents to reinforce basic theological truths. Touching these themes and praying around them in season, linking one with the other, begins to build in the mind of the child the continuity of message, the power of the story into which he has been called to live.

It is a story that has not reached its ending. It is not over. We are players on the stage of a wonderful drama. Such a view of life calls us to live beyond ourselves. It invites our children into something larger than life. It helps them to see generational continuity. They begin to see themselves as extensions of God's past and his certain future. Suddenly, they are in a line with all the great Biblical characters being a part of their past. Their family has been expanded. They are sons of Abraham by faith. The great cloud of witnesses who line the balcony of heaven are members of our extended fami-

> **Prayer Treks**
>
> A "prayer mission" is typically a local excursion. A "prayer trek" is a prayer journey that may take days or months. It combines walking and driving. Prayer treks have taken place following the trail of missionaries who left behind a string of missions on the west coast. Treks have followed the trail that Sherman left through the south on his march from Atlanta to Savannah and back through the Carolinas. Treks have followed the trail of the Crusades. A family prayer trek might retrace the steps of family history and tell the story of family faith. Prayer treks might be planned to revisit revival movements in your area, or even in the nation. Prayer treks could take the place of visiting the sites churches or even occult centers in a given region. In each case, a core group agrees to make the whole trip over a certain period of days or weeks. They may arrange to meet with others along with way who have some interest in the focus of the prayer trek. Someone will need to make a detailed account of the experiences of the group, a daily group diary.

ly. Our children are moved to play their part in carrying the drama forth into the next generation, and in doing so prayerfully.

Conclusion

Henry Grady was the editor of what is now the *Atlanta Constitution*. He became a household name and a potent political power, famous for his use of the phrase "the New South." He was considered a possible presidential running mate in the 1888 election. He died at the young age of 39, after ten years as an editor. Seven thousand people watched his funeral procession. Grady Memorial Hospital opened in 1892 fulfilling his dream of a public hospital for Atlanta.

Grady is credited with one of the three great orations in American history. The first was by Patrick Henry at Williamstown; the second, by Abraham Lincoln at Gettysburg; and the third, by Henry W. Grady at New York. Before giving the oration, Grady had been stranded by a sudden thunderstorm. Bridges had been washed out. Rivers were uncrossable. On the hillside he spotted a small cabin, knocked on the door, and found a humble family who gave him shelter for the night. Sitting at their table he watched them offer thanks. Retiring to the parlor, he observed the father with the family Bible reading to his children. Each member of the family prayed in turn around the room.

The father turned to Henry and asked him to close in prayer. Grady, whose profession was that of a wordsmith, recalled that his mouth turned to paste. There were no adequate words. The simplicity of faith and the peace of that home overwhelmed him. He stuttered and stammered.

Lying on a straw mattress that night in the darkness, he asked himself, "What made America great? Was it the massive structures in Washington? Was it the natural beauty of the continent? Was it industry or initiative? Was it freedom granted by the Constitution?" "No," he concluded. It was what he had just witnessed, the decency of common people whose lives were rooted in faith and a healthy fear of God.

The next day, he altered his plans and headed for Athens, Georgia. He spent nearly two weeks with his mother at his childhood home. He felt that his own hold on the Christian faith was lessening. "Mother," he said as he took her in his strong arms and kissed her, "I have come home to spend a week with you. I have not come merely to kiss you how-de-do and good-by…I want to go back to the old days and be your boy again…tell me the old stories about Joseph and his coat, David and his sling, Daniel and the lions, Elijah and the chariot, Elisha and the bears, and all those." And the mother told again the stories that contain the seeds of faith. He would bring the Bible and say, "Read me the story of Jesus – the stable, the shepherds, the wise men, the star, the teachings of Jesus and his desire to make the world better, His crucifixion, His ascension – and how He wants me to be a good boy."

After this renewal of faith, this return to what he believed to be the roots of our greatness as a nation, Grady went to New York to give what is regarded as one of the greatest speeches in the history of the nation.

---

1 Peter Nead, *Nead's Theological Works* (1850).
2 Matthew Henry, quoted by Lockyer, 20.
3 Bill Hull, *Revival That Transforms* (Fleming Revell Company, 1998), 38.

SECTION THREE
The Church and Prayer

CHAPTER 8
Praying in the Two Big Blessing Circles

PRAYER – HOME AND CHURCH

In establishing a prayer ministry in the church, four elements are critical – personal and at-home daily prayer; the church as a house of prayer; intercessory prayer; and prayer evangelism. First, personal and family prayer must be recovered and the church has to make a transition from being a house of praise and preaching to being a house of prayer, without displacing praise and preaching. And these two – at-home and at-church prayer – are in constant dialogue with one another. They can't exist apart from the other. These reach back and draw from the two great blessings of the Bible.

We noted earlier that in Genesis, prayer and blessing were bound together. The term *bless* is derived from the Hebrew word for *knee*. In Genesis 1:28, when God blessed 'them,' it was a picture of Adam and Eve on their knees before God – receiving the blessing that has sustained all of humanity, the blessing on marriage between a man and a woman, the blessing on the home. This is an empowering blessing. Out of it, God saves Noah's family, and the human race. Out of it, God chooses the family of Abraham, Isaac and Jacob to carry a blessing to the nations. Out of it comes the house of David, and out of David, the Messiah, a new global family of believers. God has blessed the home. It is the premier blessing in the Old Testament.

In the New Testament, as Jesus left the earth, having completed his mission, he lifted his hands, and pronounced a blessing (Lk. 24:50; Acts 2:1-4). Essentially, he moved from time into eternity, blessing. Arguably, as the high priest of heaven's tabernacle, he is blessing now. As in the Old Testament, the blessing was followed by a boundary. He commanded his disciples to go to the Upper Room and wait until they heard from heaven. He was going to pray the Father to send the comforter (Acts 1:4). And they were to create a boundary around their lives, their time, their involvement in anything else, until the Holy Spirit came. On the day of Pentecost, the impact of the blessing was felt. The Holy Spirit rolled across the Jerusalem and the Upper Room like thunder and lightning. Tongues of fire settled upon them. And the church was born in the blessing of the poured out Holy Spirit, born to be a blessing (Acts 2:1-4). Unlike the first Eve, the bride partner of Christ, the Church, had respected the boundary of obedience, waiting patiently in the Upper Room for the empowering anointing.

> A dynamic praying church must be built from the inside out, employing all four levels of prayer: the secret closet, the family altar, small group praying and finally, the congregational setting.[1]
> – Richard Burr

These two blessings – on the home and the church, both out of prayer – are the two big cogs that drive prayer ministry. You cannot have a praying church with people who only pray at church. To have a praying church, you must have praying people in praying homes. And if you have praying homes, couples who kneel before God together, to be blessed, you will always have a praying church.

There are two other critical dimensions to a praying church, and they also correspond to each another – intercession and prayer evangelism. We'll consider them in another chapter. Together, these are the four dimensions of a praying church.

1. At-Home Daily Prayer

No level of church prayer can replace daily, personal prayer. If the church is *a praying church,* a significant number among them must be *praying people.* Public prayer can't replace private prayer, and private prayer needs public prayer. While corporate prayer can't replace personal prayer, the abundance of prayer meetings in Acts shows us the value of corporate prayer. The two are connected. They fuel each other. The pastor gathers the church to pray; the father gathers the family. Personal prayer moves to couple's prayer and then to the family – until the culture of the home is transformed. It becomes a praying home, not merely a home that prays.

2. The Church at Prayer

We learn to pray by praying. It is more caught than taught. Nothing can replace being in the middle of a passionate prayer meeting. Listening to others pray, blending our voices with theirs, being infected with their passion, sharing their burden for the lost – we catch the spirit of prayer. Like taking coals of fire from the altar, we carry prayer-fire home to the privacy of our own prayer closet. A church that has people who deeply love God and intercessors with hot-hearts will always have an altar full of prayer-fire. Coming together for prayer will eventually insure that our home-altar glows red with passion for the lost and a love for the Lord. Soon we will discover that we too are coming to the public altar bringing fire with us. Others will catch our heart-fire. And a revival spirit will grow. Back and forth, between our home-altars and the church, we move.

> **WAYS TO MEASURE THE SERIOUSNESS OF THE CHURCH'S COMMITMENT TO PRAYER**
>
> 1. Prayer is included in the institutional mission statement and core values.
> 2. The consideration in engaging the pastor was not just on his preaching, but on his personal commitment to prayer. Prayer is a part of the pastor's job description.
> 3. Leadership meetings are marked by extended seasons of prayer.
> 4. There is a regular – not less than once a month – church-wide prayer service in which prayer is the main thing, if not the only thing on the agenda.
> 5. Prayer, not merely prayer requests, are a part of every worship gathering.
> 6. Members pray at home daily.
> 7. Families practice, or at least are attempting to establish, family altar experiences.
> 8. A significant number of people in the congregation are committed to prayer and demonstrate that commitment by showing up for prayer meetings.

We are not successful in prayer ministry until we have established personal, at-home, daily prayer in the lives of our members, evidenced by church-wide prayer events full of humble – but passionate – people of prayer. You must not have one without the other. Generally, you will never have one without the other.

The first two critical elements in the church prayer ministry are personal and family prayer; and then, a praying church.

The Church's Prayer Ministry

Chuck Swindoll lamented about a letter he received as chancellor of Dallas Theological Seminary. A student wrote in sincere appreciation for his education. But, he confessed that when he

9. Intercessors have been identified and are regularly engaged.
10. There is a prayer leadership team.
11. The church has a prayer room or prayer center open seven days a week, and people use it.
12. There is regular teaching and training on prayer.
13. A number of prayer groups meet during the week and are open to new members so that numerous opportunities for small group prayer take place in the course of any given week.
14. Answers to prayer are celebrated.
15. The church staff pray together at least weekly.
16. The elders or church council pray together.
17. There is a definitive prayer evangelism focus, including prayer for those who do not yet know Christ in a saving and satisfying way.
18. Money is appropriated in the church budget to support the prayer ministry of the church.
19. Men are being encouraged to pray and regularly gather for prayer. Intercession is not merely a women's phenomenon.
20. Youth and children are being discipled in prayer.

came "he was deeply in love with Jesus Christ; but when he left, he had fallen more in love with the biblical text…he left loving the Bible more than he loved his Savior."[2] Sadly, that could be said of far too many Bible Colleges and Seminaries where *prayer* is ancillary, something assumed – not a part of the curriculum or appropriately valued.

Prayer brings Jesus back to the center of the believer's life! Our churches have become "houses of preaching" instead of "houses of prayer." Frank Lauback charges, "Evangelical Christianity is lost unless it discovers that the center and power of its divine service is prayer, not preaching."[3] Prayer enhances preaching, and preaching should drive us to prayer. Yet, as Frederick Heiler noted, "Not speech about God, but speech to God; not the preaching of the revelation of God, but direct intercourse with God is, strictly speaking, the worship of God." George Buttrick got it right – *"Corporate prayer is the heart of corporate worship."*

The Reformation sought to ground the church on objective truth. It made the pulpit central. Buttrick says, "When the book is made central, prayer may become an appendage of scribal interpretations. When preaching is made central, prayer...may become only an introduction and conclusion to the sermon. The heart of religion is in prayer...prayer must go through the rite, Scripture, symbolism, and sermon, as light though a window."[4] Oswald Chambers declared, "Prayer does not equip us for the greater works – prayer is the greater work."[5]

Praying Corporately

Many congregations have never learned to allow the Holy Spirit to move them along together in an unhurried manner, just

---

Circles of Prayer

Circles of prayer are a good way to engage the entire congregation in prayerful moments. Some churches call this the "Take Five!" exercise. Make a group, right in the pews, but limit it to five. Post on the sanctuary screen potential prayer focuses. Be careful not to overwhelm the congregation with too many. Balance the needs. Don't just post typical "prayer requests, sicknesses, hospitalizations, etc." List nations, among them unreached peoples that need prayer. Issues that should be offered to God affecting our nation. List missionaries. List area businesses and community needs. Ask the group of five to choose five needs for which to pray. Then give them time to pray for other needs not noted on the screen. Encourage one or two in each circle to lead out in prayer. Don't force everyone in the circle to pray out loud. And yet, such prayer experiences begin to nudge us toward learning to be vocal and expressive in our prayers.

waiting in prayer. One prays, then another. A season of quiet comes. One has a word, another confirms it. Prayers are offered, each following the other, as if everyone were reading from the same script. The many voices become one, corporately learning and listening in prayer. In such moments, the Spirit comes. There is no program. No agenda. No script. The church has gathered to meet God and He shows up.

Other people pray in ways you and I would never pray. That is why we need to hear one another pray. You may express my heart with language I did not have. You may be bolder and more vulnerable before God than I would dare to be. You touch something in prayer that resonates in me, that rattles my soul, making me wonderfully uncomfortable. In unhurried seasons, we find others praying our thoughts. In these times of vulnerability and transparency, an honest hunger for God coupled with genuine repentance and humility allows the Spirit to pierce the hardest heart. Tears come. Brokenness follows. We are all in the presence of a holy God. The pursuit and spiritual yearning of one feeds the longing in the heart of another. The capacity for humility in one is a quiet and convicting indictment of the arrogance in another. We are "iron sharpening iron." And yet all this happens in a way that avoids conflict and confrontation. Such prayer is not a mere transaction with God; it is transformational. "The only way up is down."[6] Performance-based Christianity is out; authenticity and genuineness are in.

While the heart of prayer is communion with God, that is not the *all* of prayer. It involves *intercession* – prayer for others. It involves *petition* – prayer for our own needs. It involves *thanksgiving* – a humble gratitude that stimulates faith by a regular review of God's gracious history in our lives. Thanksgiving is sometimes a discipline. It wakes up a cold heart. It systematically surveys the past and looks for traces of God's intervention. It marks the path we have taken and signs of God's hand at work in providing and directing, in protecting.

Praying With Variety

We are to pray *"with all kinds of prayers"* (Ephesians 6:18 NIV). A good prayer ministry demands variety. Don't allow the prayer life of the church to get into a rut. Pray "with all prayer." Pray with others. Pray aloud at the same time. The fervency of multiple voices lifted to God all at once, like a symphony, is a component of passionate praying that the entire global Church is now increasingly embracing. In American Pentecostal Churches, the practice was common a few generations ago; now it is waning, if not dying. But in other evangelical circles, it is becoming common. Such prayer is rich with intensity. It is ardent and fiery. But it is not the only way to pray.

What we sometimes call "corporate prayer" isn't corporate. It is individuals, each finding a place and praying in the same room aloud together. That is a legitimate and passionate context of prayer. But corporate prayer is different. It puts us all on the same page, on the same topic, praying in the same direction. We need to learn to pray with all prayer:

- **Concert Prayer** – Everyone lifting their voice together, praying aloud, as a symphony.

- **Congregational Prayers** – Several people pray, one after another, as others listen and agree.

- **Covenant Prayers** – Give voice to His love for us and our love for him. Prayers that reaffirm our covenant, that express our commitment.

- **Directed praying** – A focus for prayer is offered followed by a season of prayer, five to ten minutes, followed by a

> **Nursery Prayer**
>
> Nurseries have become places to park babies. But the church was never called to "child care" as much as it has been called to "child cultivation." Turn the nursery into a prayer room. Don't allow a hired outsider who is not even a believer to tend the lambs. As babies are rocked, instruct nursery workers to sing to them and pray over them. Claim every child that is committed to the care of the nursery. Pray that from this moment, God will mark the steps of their lives. Nursery intercessors might want to take pictures of each baby and continue to pray for them even if parents don't return to church. A prayer is an eternal matter. And a simple prayer prayed over a child may direct the path of that child in an unfathomable and mysterious way. Bless the children. Pray over the babies. At the toddler age, pray with them. How tragic that toddlers come to associate church with playing rather than praying. Teach the little ones to pray. Recite prayers to them. Have them memorize the prayers. Nurseries are now sometimes filled with decorations that have little to do with faith. Make sure the images in your nursery build the child's inner faith library with visual representations that they will carry for a lifetime.

second focus and another short season of prayer. This deliberate process continues until a variety of needs have been considered. Allow for openness to the Holy Spirit on any matter in order for the prayer concern to be thoroughly explored. We rush through prayer needs. We simply repeat the need to God with bowed heads and closed eyes, but that is not praying. Good prayer explores a matter in consultation with God.

- ♦ **Intercessory Prayers** – Prayer for the lost, the unsaved; unreached people groups; for kings and nations; for the peace of Jerusalem; for family and friends; for pastors and Christian workers; for those in authority; for our city and counties, regions and states; for neighbors and work associates; for brothers and sisters in Christ; for the persecuted church; for businesses that bless the community; for enterprises that do harm – that God would close them; for the redemption of the land; for the youth of the city; for the children – that they not grow up in a nation that has turned its back on God; for the widow and the orphan; for those stricken with disease; for the oppressed and forsaken; for those in prison or on probation.

- **Pastoral Prayers** – The pastor prays and the congregation allows him to intercede in their behalf, listening and silently agreeing.

- **Prayers of Agreement** – Each person prays in succession, first one, and then another, each building and loading into the prayers that came before. It is praying as the spirit leads about first one issue, some concern, and then another matter.

- **Prayers of Praise** – Focused beyond His acts on the character and nature of God. He does what He does because of who He is.

- **Prayers of Repentance** – Reflect our pursuit of character before His Holiness.

- **Prayers of Thanksgiving** – Prayer for the specific acts and blessings of God.

- **Silence** – Here we experience the holy hush of His Presence. No one speaks. No tongues or interpretation. No prophetic words. Only the piercing voice of the Spirit speaking into each heart.

- **Small groups** – Each group or all groups focused on some need.

- **Waiting Prayer** – Laced with the operation of the gifts, prayer is offered. Then there is patient waiting. Then, perhaps, there is a word from the Lord or a Scripture [which should always be considered to have the force of prophecy – a word to edify, comfort or exhort: I Corinthians 14:1-2] to be considered, then more prayer and discernment until, by the gracious working of the Spirit, we reach an end and sense a breakthrough.

What we need in the church is not merely more prayer activities, but a "culture of prayer." The goal should be for the entire church to embrace prayer as the norm![7]

In an earlier book, *Transforming the Church into a House of Prayer*, are listed numerous ways to enrich the corporate prayer experience. Here is an abbreviation of that list.

1. <u>Make prayer a prominent feature</u> in your <u>Sunday Morning</u> Worship service.

Suggestions for Prayer and Petition[8]

1. We must pray in faith, not doubting (Hebrews 11:6; Matthew 17:20; Mark 11:23-24; James 1:6). (See Richards, 166)
2. We must pray with clean hands and a pure heart. (Psalm 66:18; Proverbs 28:9; Isaiah 59:1-2).
3. We must pray out of and with a forgiving heart. Unforgiveness is a fatal flaw in one's prayer life. (Matthew 6:12-15; 18:21-35; Mark 11:25-26; James 5:14-16).
4. We must pray with humility.
5. We must must pray with a heart committed to unity and healthy relationships. (Matthew 5:23-24; 18:19; 1 Peter 3:1-7: This latter passage deals with hindered prayers in the context of marriage where an unhealthy relationship has developed, or there is little or no respect between partners.)
6. We must not be double-minded.
7. God honors effectual, fervent, and passionate prayer. (Luke 11:5-8; 18:1-8; James 5:16)
8. We must be sincere. In biblical prayer, there is no hollow *pathos*, no tears for the sake of tears, no beating of the beast, no showy attention-getting behavior. Nor is their a need for flattering offered to God with mere words. God prefers childlike simplicity. Further, the private prayers of the people are to reflect the character of public prayers. In other words, as we are with others in prayer, so we are when alone in prayer. Public prayer must have private roots. When praise is offered it must be sincere.

2. <u>Include a pastoral prayer</u> or a pastoral blessing. As a priest, as a pastor, and take your people to God. Bring God to them. Bless them.

3. <u>Have the congregation pray</u> corporate prayers together. Put them on the video screen. Pray and pause, allowing for personal moments between the corporate prayers.

4. <u>Sing about prayer</u>. There are great hymns with prayer language that will linger with us all week.

5. <u>Preach on prayer</u>. Then <u>practice it</u>.

6. <u>Allow for seasons of congregational prayer</u>. Bring the whole church forward. Wait before the Lord.

7. <u>Encourage individual prayer</u> in the altar. Reestablish the notion of tarrying before the Lord.

8. <u>Let the children pray</u>.

9. <u>Call men</u> forward. Charge fathers with the task of being the priests of their homes. Bless them. Tell them that they are equal to the task of leading prayer with their families.

10. <u>Change the way you manage prayer requests</u>. Don't talk about prayer needs. Pray them, spontaneously. Say, "You may now pray out the needs of your loved ones?"

11. Establish a prayer request box. Occasionally, encourage members to take a handful of requests out. Pray over them and then place them back into the box.

12. Don't forget to <u>give thanks</u> for answers to prayer. Keep a record of God's provisions, a diary of God's dashing actions in behalf of your people.

13. <u>Feature prayer testimonies</u> as a regular part of the service. Show video clips that feature answered prayers and encourage praying.

14. <u>Pray for a different church in your city every week</u>. Become kingdom-focused and not merely congregation focused.

15. <u>Establish a prayer room</u>.

16. Encourage simultaneous intercession during worship.
16. Designate intercessors to pray before and during each worship service.
17. Hang prayer banners in the church.[9] Make them visual reminders of prayer needs. Make the banners prayer stations. Have the people occasionally go to the banners during prayer time.
18. Have special prayer services – a solemn assembly, a concert of prayer, family prayer, men's prayer, women's prayer, a youth prayer event.
19. Have a 15-minute pre-service prayer meeting.
20. Have a church-wide prayer meeting once a week if possible, and not less than once a month.[10]

Here are some additional ideas to move prayer toward the center of church life.

1. Pastors, staff and other leaders must model prayer. The disciples became men of prayer because Jesus was a man of prayer. The Acts church became a praying church, because the 120 apostles and lead-laypersons were praying people.
2. Establish a regular church-wide prayer meeting. Emphasize its importance. Mix time for personal prayer and corporate prayer. Direct the various prayer points for any given evening.
3. Create a space for prayer in the church facility – a prayer room. Make it accessible seven days a week. Schedule prayer team members to be present and use the room. Make it open to all.
4. Appoint a prayer leadership team. Have enough members on the team to cover the key areas of nurturing personal and family prayer; networking and training intercessors; integrating prayer into every ministry of the church; proliferating prayer groups; managing prayer needs; rapid

response prayer teams; prayer counselors/altar workers; healing teams; pastor's prayer partners; prayer evangelism; coordination of the prayer room or center; prayer training.

5. Call the men to prayer – teach and emphasize the family altar; prayer with wives and children; the power of blessing; the role of priestly leadership in the home.

6. Identify intercessors. Train them. Team them. Debrief them. Direct them.

7. Pray the Sanctuary. Sweep your sanctuary and bathe it in prayer. Prayer-walk every foot of your facility. Invite God's presence.

8. Sponsor a School of Prayer or regular training on prayer.[11]

9. Enlist the whole church to join the "Pastor's Prayer Team." On the day of the month corresponding to their birthday, have them take their place on the wall.

10. Do prayer-walks, prayer-missions, new stretching prayer experiences to push prayer out into the harvest field.

11. Establish a Wailing Wall. Post pictures and names of friends and family who need a closer relationship with Christ. Weep at the wall. Ask God to reveal himself to these loved ones.

12. Keep prayer literature and resources flowing into and through the congregation. Focus on materials that will support and enrich the personal and family prayer experiences.

13. Emphasize answers to prayer.

14. Vary the prayer experiences. Introduce new ways to pray. Introduce tools for enriching the church prayer life, and personal prayer.

15. Proliferate prayer groups – a prayer group for and around every burden and cause. Small groups of five to twelve. Train the leaders. Monitor their effectiveness.[12]

Creating a Circle of Prayer for the Pastor

1. Recruit Prayer Partners for the Pastor. It is inadequate to say "the whole church is praying for the pastor." Get commitments.
2. Have the prayer partners take a day of the week or one day a month (anniversary or birthday date, 23rd, i.e.). Make a calendar of who is praying on any day.
3. Distribute a weekly "Prayer Points" bulletin.
4. Encourage the pastor to be open to prayer – to receive "the gift of prayer" from intercessors and prayer partners who stop by the office.
5. Build a library for prayer partners and intercessors to use.
6. Have a team of intercessors assigned to each Sunday for special prayer for the service.
7. Have Sunday School classes rotate and once a month, or quarterly, pray for the pastor. "Today is our day to pray a special prayer covering for our pastor."
8. Make sure the elders or council designate time in their monthly board meeting to pray for the pastor. This is one of their chief roles, if not the chief one. Don't allow this to be either a formal matter or a flighty thing. If the whole session were spent in prayer for the pastor, no better use of time could be found. An elder team or pastor's council who is not praying for the pastor can never lead the church effectively.
9. Encourage the members who prayed for the pastor during the week to give him a "thumbs up" sign as he enters the pulpit to preach each Sunday.
10. Make sure you share testimonies of answered prayer and intervention.

The two big cogs in the prayer ministry wheels of the church are personal, at-home, transformational praying; and, the church gathered, not for preaching or teaching, but for prayer. These are rooted in, and draw on the two great blessings in Scripture. The first constituted the home, and the second, the church.

Between these two – personal and corporate prayer – stand the couple's prayer life, the family altar, and small group prayer. Every believer should be in multiple prayer connections. Daily personal prayer. Daily, certainly regular and frequent prayer connections as a couple. A family altar. Participation in some small prayer group. And regular times when the congregation gathers to pray and wait on the Lord, as in Acts 2, for His continued blessing. Beyond these, look for ways to join congregations in prayer; to call believers in a city to prayer.

As Billy Graham often says, "The three most important things you can do are to pray, pray, pray!"

Praying in the Two Big Blessing Circle

1. Richard Burr, *Developing Your Secret Closet of Prayer* (Christian Publications, 1998), 19. Burr's four levels are not the same as the "Four Dimensional Elements" here. His levels are part of the larger whole. Burr's closet and family altar are inside dimension one – personal and family prayer. Burr's small group and congregational prayer are dimension two – the church at prayer. In addition to these, special attention should be given to mobilizing intercessors and also to missional prayer.
2. Chuck Swindoll, *So, You Want To Be Like Christ?* (Nashville, TN: W Publishing Group, a division of Thomas Nelson, 2005), 40.
3. Frank Lauback, *Prayer-the Mightiest Force in the World* (Westwood, NJ: Spire Books-Fleming H. Revell, 1946), 50.
4. George Buttrick, "Leading Public Prayer," *The Contemporaries Meet The Classics on Prayer*, ed. Leonard Allen (West Monroe, LA: Howard Publishing, 2003), 238.
5. Oswald Chambers, "The Key of the Greater Work," *The Contemporaries Meet The Classics on Prayer*, ed. Leonard Allen (West Monroe, LA: Howard Publishing, 2003), 257.
6. Herbert Lockyer, *All the Prayers of the Bible* (Grand Rapids, MI: Zonservan, 1959), 25.
7. P. Douglas Small, *Transforming the Church into a House of Prayer* (Cleveland, TN: Pathway Press, 2006), 51.
8. Larry Richards, *Every Prayer and Petition in the Bible* (Thomas Nelson, 2004).
9. You can purchase prayer banners from Alive Ministries: PROJECT PRAY at www.alivepublications.org.
10. For a fuller description of these ideas, see the book: P. Douglas Small, *Transforming Your Church into a House of Prayer*, 93-101.
11. Alive Ministries: PROJECT PRAY offers various Schools of Prayer. Learn more at www.projectpray.org.
12. For a fuller description of these ideas, see the book: P. Douglas Small, *Transforming Your Church into a House of Prayer*.

CHAPTER 9
The Church – A House of Prayer

According to my humble judgment, the greatest need of the present-day church is prayer. Prayer should be the vital breath of the church, but right now it is gasping for air...the church goes forward on its knees. Maybe one of the reasons the church is not going forward today is because it's not in a position to go forward. We are not on our knees in prayer.

– J. Vernon McGee

The Church and Power

E. M. Bounds says,

The great lack of modern religion is the spirit of devotion. We hear sermons in the same spirit with which we listen to a lecture or a speech. We visit the house of God just as if it were a common place, on the level with a theater, the lecture room, or the forum. We look at the minister of God not as the divinely called man of God, but merely as a sort of public speaker...We handle sacred things just as if they were the things of the world...Oh, how the spirit of true and genuine devotion would radically change all this for the better![1]

A "feeble, lively, showy religious activity" can never compensate when the "spirit of genuine, heartfelt devotion is strangely lacking."

Prayer and the Miraculous

The book of Acts explodes with miraculous power. Jerusalem is on its heels, reeling from the impact of the resurrected Christ, alive by the Spirit, and working through the Church. In the first five chapters, Luke seems to layer one miracle feature after another. There are eight miracle mentions – Acts 1:9; 2:1-4, 43; 3:1-10; 4:31; 5:1-11, 12-16, 19. In both Acts 2:43 and 5:12-16, numerous miracles may have occurred. Notice how these interweave with prayer.[2]

PRAYER	POWER
The command to tarry in prayer	the miracle of the Ascension (Acts 1:8-9)
The church obediently obeys Christ and persists in prayer	the fire falls, the wind of Heaven rolls in, they are filled with the Spirit (Acts 2:1-4)
The church continues in prayer	signs and wonders abound (Acts 2:42-43)
Peter and John go to prayer	God heals the man at the temple gate (Acts 3:1-8)
The church gathers for prayer under threat from the officials	the place where they assembled shakes in response to the Spirit (Acts 4:31)

Prayer and Power

The miraculous ascension is coupled with the command to wait prayerfully in the upper room (Acts 1:9). The Holy Spirit comes to a room full of united, praying believers (Acts 1-4). The "signs and wonders" happen in the context of a praying church gladly receiving the Word (Acts 2: 41-43). The lame man is healed as Peter and John head to a prayer meeting (Acts 3:1-10). After being threatened and told not to mention the name of Jesus, the church gathers for prayer and the room trembles (Acts 4:31).

Here is prayer on top of prayer. These are powerful demonstrations of God's presence out of prayer. This is the Acts church. When church growth slowed and internal strife manifested, the correctional strategy was a reinvestment in prayer. *"We will give ourselves continually to prayer and the ministry of the Word."* (Acts 6:4) With that, division was healed and church growth resumed.

Years ago, the order was given that no more meetings by Christian Protestants would be allowed in the city of Osaka, Japan. The officials resisted all attempts to rescind their ban. Two Christian leaders did the only thing they knew to do – pray! A young Japanese girl was sent to call them to supper. As she entered the room where they were praying, she too fell under the power of prayer. One of the wives of the leaders, not understanding the delay, went to seek her husband. She, too, came under the spirit of intercession. That night, in defiance of the order to cease their meetings, they opened the mission hall. As soon as the meeting began, God came. Two sons of the city officials came to the altar that night and were saved. The next morning, the leaders got word, "Go on with your meetings; you will not be interrupted." The daily newspaper reported the reversal in boxcar letters – "THE CHRISTIANS' GOD CAME TO TOWN LAST NIGHT!"[3]

> But have we Holy Ghost power – power that restricts the devil's power, pulls down strongholds and obtains promises? Daring delinquents will be damned if they are not delivered from the devil's dominion. What has hell to fear other than a God-anointed, prayer-powered church?"
> – Leonard Ravenhill

Revival of Prayer

Set aside a whole week for prayer. Open the church each morning and evening. Have it open during the day. Have a different focus each evening – men's prayer evening, women's prayer evening, couple's prayer, family prayer, mission-evangelism praying, prayer for the lost, an anointing service for healing, prayer for business owners and workers. Join with a nearby church, and make that evening one in which leaders and members pray for one another's churches and ministries. Have one evening in which the church meets at some strategic site for a prayer walk or a prayer mission. Have a night of thanksgiving praying. Make sure each evening is full of substance. Allow the Holy Spirit to rewrite the order of every service, but go with a well-planned and thought-out approach to prayer. Have visuals ready or handouts to use as resources in the prayer gatherings. Don't just pray for people, have the people pray. Have one night in which the families stay home and pray together. Give them ideas for the evening – Scripture readings, samples of prayers, a video that can be viewed, prayer exercises, songs to sing together, symbolic acts they can do (the Passover was a house-based event loaded with symbolic action). This one night could be the beginning of family worship in many of your homes. That alone could bring a revival. This would be a good week to emphasize the establishment of a personal place of prayer, the creation of a personal or family altar in the home. And if possible, the dedication of a prayer closet. Teach on the value of at-home, personal, daily prayer. Teach on the idea of the prayer closet.[1] Have people share their stories of creating and beginning to use their prayer closet or family altar. Don't make this a week of teaching – make it a week of prayer. Encourage members to fast TV during the week. Make the entire eight days – Sunday-to-Sunday, a time of consecration.

---

1 Learn more: P. Douglas Small, *The Prayer Closet - Creating a Personal Prayer Room* (Kannapolis, NC: Alive Publications, 2015).

Prayer and Witness

"What does this mean?" asked the Jerusalem crowd in response to the Holy Spirit so evidently manifest. It means, Peter explained, that Jesus, who had been crucified and buried, was not dead: *"His soul was not left in the grave"* (Acts 2:27). He is *"by the right hand of God, exalted"* (v. 33). The empowerment of the Spirit on the bride, the Church, his followers, is proof that hHe is alive. Authorities who had sought to silence his message and stop his miracles were now faced with a dilemma. Instead of one man with a dissident message or even twelve, now there were 120 behaving like Jesus. *"This same Jesus"* is both *"Lord and Christ,"* Peter exclaimed (v. 36). He had promised to return in a way that the disciples would see him, but the world would not. Through the agency of the Holy Spirit, Jesus was back. This time, he was not merely with his disciples; he was in them (John 14:17). *"Greater things shall you do because I go to the Father."*

How do you fight a ghost? How do you destroy the indestructible? Emboldened by his resurrection and the indwelling Spirit, the disciples were now as fearless as he had been. They talked like him. Acted like him. Did miracles like him. The Ghost – the Holy Ghost – changed them in more ways than one. Christ was evident in their *proclamation*, but there had also been a second *incarnation*. Christ was in them in love and truth, as well as in power.

True Pentecost demands Christ-likeness. The greatest sign and wonder is a transformed church. If people see supernatural *power* but fail to find supernatural *fruit*, they will only be disillusioned. Signs and wonders are advertisements to the fact that Jesus is alive. They are invitations into Jesus, into *the body* of Christ, and into a new way to live.

Prayer and Character

But miracles are not the only signs and wonders. The character that emerges in the church itself is miraculous. The disciples continued steadfastly in teaching, learning, growing. Their *koinonia* was exceptional: it was a family-like fellowship. They shared. They prayed together in the homes of one another. Praise resounded in the streets. Daily, people were joining the movement. The Holy Spirit had changed the character of the church itself. There was an absence of clamor for position. Humility characterized them.

POWER	**CHARACTER**
	They were all in one accord and in one mind…(Acts 2:1).
Suddenly there came a sound from Heaven, a mighty rushing wind, tongues of fire…and they were filled with the Spirit…a multitude gathered (vv. 4, 6).	
Fear came on every soul …signs and wonders were done…(v. 43)	*and they had all things in common; They sold possessions and gave to men in need…*
	…they continued daily with one accord, in the temple, from house to house…with gladness…singleness of heart… praising God, finding favor with the people (vv. 43-47)
And when they had prayed, the place was shaken… they were filled with the Holy Ghost, and spoke the word with boldness…	*And those who believed were of one heart and soul, neither did any say that the things he possessed was his own… (vv. 31-32)*
And with great power gave the apostles	

The Church - A House of Prayer

Witness of the resurrection...
Great grace was on them...
(v. 33)

Neither was there any who lacked...the possessors of lands or houses sold them and gave the proceeds laying them at the apostle's feet...(vv. 34-35)

Ananias and Sapphira sold a possession And kept back part of the price... they lied to the Holy Spirit...

Peter said, Satan has filled your heart...And Ananias fell dead then she fell... and great fear came upon all... and signs and wonders were wrought among the people... and believers were added ...the sick were brought to the streets...

A multitude came out of cities round about... and they were healed, Everyone of them.
(5:1-3, 5, 10-12, 14-16)

They laid hands on the apostles and put them in the common prison...but the Angel of the Lord opened the prison doors and brought them out, and said, "Go stand and speak in the temple..."

We ought to obey God rather than man...they beat them... and they rejoiced that they were counted worthy to suffer for his name...and they ceased not to teach...Acts (v. 18-20, 29, 40-42).

John Newton once said,

> If two angels were to receive at the same moment a commission from God, one to go down and rule the earth's grandest empire, the other to go and sweep the streets of the meanest village, it would be a matter of entire indifference to each which service fell to his lot, the post of ruler or the post of scavenger; for the joy of the angels lies only in obedience to God's will.[4]

E. M. Bounds declared,

> Humility retires itself from the public gaze. It does not seek publicity nor hunt for high places, neither does it care for prominence...it is given to self-depreciation. It never exalts itself in the eyes of others nor even in the eyes of itself.[5]

What Jerusalem witnessed in these transformed Christ-followers was something greater than the street miracles, a miracle even more profound – people of one heart and mind, caring and sharing, praying daily, loving their enemies, living in grace, giving witness to the reality of another world, to the resurrection of Christ from the dead. They had been freed from things. They gave. They liquidated their assets to finance the first great surge of the gospel. They became a sharing, caring community committed to the mission of Christ. Agape flowed. Fellowship was sweet. Joy was abundant. It seemed that the whole city wanted to become members of the church.

In our day, the tendency, at least among some Pentecostals, is to emphasize supernatural power without an equal emphasis upon supernatural character. Evangelical non-Pentecostals sometimes err in the opposite direction. Both are essential. Paul, in the discussion about Pentecostal gifts (1 Corinthians 12-14), introduces the topic of 'agape.' The essence of character is unconditional love. Power manifestations without character are confusing. Fire without fruit is less than the Pentecostal church evidence in Acts. The judgment of Ananias and Sapphira is testimony to that demand.

The Church - A House of Prayer

Truth must be a lifestyle, not merely a stated doctrine. Without integrity our message is hollow. As Dr. Joe Aldrich, founder of the pastor's prayer movement was fond of saying, "The gospel rides on the beauty of the transformed church. We don't have the message. We are the message." What we proclaim, we must incarnate. Our lives speak louder than our words.

Jesus, by the enabling work of the Spirit, is the message in the Book of Acts.

- *"Silver and gold have I none,"* Peter said, *"but in the name of Jesus..."* (3:6), rise and walk.
- In Acts 1:11; 2:20 – *Jesus* is coming back.
- In Acts 2:22 – *Jesus* is <u>a man of miracles</u>, wonders and signs, crucified and yet alive. He can't be killed.
- In Acts 2:32-33 – *Jesus* <u>has risen</u>. He is exalted. The supernatural coming of the Spirit is evidence. Our purpose is to give witness to his resurrection and exaltation.
- In Acts 2:36 – *Jesus* <u>is the King</u>, reigning in exile, the Lord and Messiah now sitting at the Father's right hand.
- In Acts 2:38 – Since that is true, <u>sinful men must repent</u>.
- In Acts 3:6 – The name of *Jesus* <u>has healing power</u>.
- In Acts 3:13-16 – *Jesus*, the Prince of Life, crucified, <u>has now been glorified</u> by the God of Abraham, Isaac and Jacob.
- In Acts 4:10 – <u>Salvation is in the name of</u> *Jesus*, alone.
- In Acts 4:18-20 – <u>Silence</u>, about *Jesus*, <u>is impossible</u> in view of the things seen and heard.
- In Acts 4:26-30 – When the leadership of the whole nation had lined up against *Jesus*, in the church, <u>prayer</u> was offered <u>for the boldness to speak the name of</u> *Jesus* as a witness to His life.

The Church understood their role was to give witness to the

resurrection of Christ. In every chapter in Acts 1-5, the theme of witness emerges.

- Acts 1:8 – you shall be witnesses.
- Acts 2:32; 3:15; 5:32 – we are witnesses.
- Acts 4:33 – with great power gave the apostles witness of the resurrection.

Not only are they witnesses of Jesus, they are no longer intimidated by either the crucifying power of the Romans or the authority of the religious establishment. They boldly offer their witness.

- In Acts 2:12-14, 36 – Peter stands up and boldly answers the accusations.
- In Acts 3:4-7 – The disciples boldly and openly pray for needs in the name of Jesus.
- In Acts 3:11-16 – Peter, knowing the potential consequences, attributes the miracle of the lame man to Jesus and asserts that it is proof of both the resurrection and glorification of Christ in heaven.
- In Acts 4:29, 31 – When censored for speaking in the name of Jesus, the church prays for boldness to continue to speak despite the threats.
- In Acts 5:1-3 – Peter boldly confronts compromise in the church, even when it is a wealthy and influential couple such as Ananias and Sapphira.
- In Acts 5:29 – When threatened by authorities, the disciples declare their ultimate intention to obey God rather than man.
- In Acts 5:42 – Having been beaten, and yet escaping with their lives from authorities, they do not tone down their activities. Daily, openly and publicly, they do not stop preaching and teaching about Jesus.

The boldness comes from the Holy Spirit, through prayer. Prayer invites an anointing that demonstrates to a watching world that Jesus is not dead. He is alive. Still, the underemphasized miracle in the book of Acts is the transformation of the lives of the believers and the community that was cradled in love and defined by truth. That community – holy, humble, unified, full of the Spirit – was a miracle. We need a miracle that transforms the character of the contemporary church. A miracle that makes us Christ-like. A miracle that loads our branches with the fruit of the Spirit – love, joy, peace, longsuffering, gentleness [kindness], goodness, faithfulness, meekness [strength under control, a gentle disposition], temperance [self-control]. A miracle that makes us gracious without compromising truth. A miracle that causes us to walk truth as much as we talk truth.

If America is going to see revival, it must first see Christ in a transformed church. And if America is going to repent of its many sins, it must first hear the church repenting of its many sins. Judgment, we learn from Acts 5, begins in the house of the Lord. If our unsaved friends and families saw us weeping about the condition of our own lives before the holiness of God, they might say to themselves, *"If the righteous scarcely be saved, where does the sinner and the ungodly stand?"* (1 Peter 4:17-18). We will do more to promote conviction of sin by our humble response to God's holiness than by our attempts to coach a sinful culture into repentance. Our tear-stained faces, about things our worldly friends might consider slight sins, our conscientious desire to please God, should cause them to say, "If he needs to repent, I need massive change in my life." In the bright light of God's holiness, our righteousness is always a dingy gray. Holy people are humble people.

Prayer and Unity

> Nothing tends more to cement the hearts of Christians than praying together. Never do they love one another so well as when they witness the outpouring of each other's hearts in prayer.[6]

Getting Started with A Prayer Ministry

1. **DO IT** – <u>Pray. Don't talk about it. Do it</u>. Pray before you plan. Pray before you do anything else. Above all, let prayer lead the way in developing a prayer ministry. Tarry in prayer. The flesh will want to plan it into being. The Spirit will want to prayer it into being. Pray for prayer – a spirit of intercession. Pray for pray-ers – an army of prayer warriors. Pray for wisdom and direction in prayer. Pray for God to identify prayer leaders. Pray for a passion for the lost. Pray for God's unique design for the prayer ministry of your church.

2. **ENVISION IT** – <u>Pray aloud</u>, "By faith, I see ..." Have the participants fill in the blanks. Let prayer, bathed in faith, quicken your hearts with the possibilities for prayer ministry. Don' hurry. Wait in prayer.

3. **RECORD IT** – <u>Have someone record the ideas</u>. "By faith, I see ... us prayer walking the city ... (another) ... with healing teams ... praying regularly for the mayor." Some things envisioned in prayer may be immediately forthcoming. Some may only unfold after years of faithful persistence. A record might encourage latecomers to the process that God had a huge mission in mind from the beginning.

4. **TALK IT UP** – Keep sharing ideas for prayer. <u>Enlarge the circle</u>. As more people are exposed to the things stirring in the hearts of a few, the Lord will call others into the process. And the vision will become clear.

5. **PRIORITIZE IT** – Begin to separate the ideas about which you have prayed and talked into prioritized categories – do these immediately. Do as soon as possible. Do later. Wait on the Lord. <u>Develop an action plan</u>. Keep committing ideas and plans to prayer. Keep it fluid.

6. **STEWARD IT** – By now, <u>a core group</u> has emerged who want to see a prayer team become a reality. Some will have a passion for prayer, but not be gifted as organizers and leaders. Ideally, you want an intercessor who is also a gifted leader with evidenced maturity to serve as your team leader. Team is a key word. This is not a one-person job. <u>A prayer ministry demands a team</u>. Designate the team members. Keep the roles loosely defined in the discovery and exploratory phases.

Stephen Olford, the great preacher, said, "I came to the conclusion that the two outstanding conditions for revival are unity and prayer."[7] J. Hudson Taylor declared, "The spirit of prayer is, in essence, the spirit of revival."[8] Prayer connects the Church with its Head, the Lord Jesus Christ (Colossians 2:19). Jesus Christ alone is able to fill his church with his own life and power. He alone is able to take immediate control of his church and run it from heaven by his Spirit.

The Church is more than a community that shares doctrine. It is a community of life and love in union with our Lord Himself. We can meet with Him and talk to Him in prayer. His church began as a prayer meeting (Acts 1:14) and it is sustained in prayer. Just as children share life and love with their parents, so the church family should share life and love with Christ. The gift of grace is a life-giving bonding agent. But that relationship demands nurture. It can be neglected, strained and even severed. A parent who has lost the love of a child is left hurt and empty. The unresponsive church grieves God in the same way. Love, even God's love, can be rejected. The church at Ephesus neglected its first love. Christ warned it to repent or he would remove the light from its midst (Revelation 2:4-5). The Laodicea church became lukewarm, and Christ said he was ready to spew it out of his mouth (Revelation 3:16).

THREE KINDS OF CHURCHES

There are three kinds of churches. Some churches pray when there is a *crisis*. Other churches have a *prayer ministry among other ministries*. Finally, there are churches that seek to bring prayer to the *center of every ministry*, to everything the church strives to do and be. They want to become a house of prayer for the nations.[9]

First, we can no longer pray only about our needs. Second, prayer can never be a program in the church. Further, prayer min-

7. **WORK IT** – Transform the vision, with its priority categories, into <u>action steps</u>. Don't stop praying. <u>Pray and plan</u>. <u>Work and pray</u>! Keep enlarging the circle of people meeting to move the prayer process forward.
8. **GROW IT** – With the core vision given the group in prayer, now <u>expose yourself to all kinds of ideas</u>. Don't copy other prayer ministries, but do <u>learn</u> from them. Assign each of your team members a different book to read on prayer ministries – not just prayer. Come together. Have them share insights. Secure a copy of these publications: *Transforming Your Church into a House of Prayer; The Praying Church Resource Guide* (a 700-page collage of prayer ideas); *The Praying Church Made Simple* – all available from Alive Publications. These resources focus only on prayer, but on developing a prayer ministry.
9. **EVALUATE IT** – In light of what you are learning, how balanced is your plan? How likely is it that you can accomplish all your goals in the time-line you might have set? Have other prayer ministry leaders from other churches <u>assess your plan</u>. Get pastoral approval. Make sure your team is on board.
10. **EXECUTE IT** – Even as you <u>put your plan in action</u>, keep it flexible. You learn by doing. As you conduct prayer events, you will see gaps in prayer theology and practice. Teach and train into those gaps. Then test the learning by another doing event. Build slowly - teach and execute; train and deploy. Set reasonable goals. Make them measurable. Expect resistance. This is a marathon, not a sprint.

istry cannot be a department among other departments. There cannot be a choice – if you sing, join our choir; if you teach, be a part of our Christian education program; if you love youth, work with our young people; and, oh yes, if you like to pray, we have a prayer ministry. Such an approach is doomed to failure. Our third choice is a model for prayer ministry that seeds prayer into every department of the church until there is a praying staff, with praying elders, and praying youth leaders, praying nursery workers and praying families. Everything we do must be bathed in prayer.[10] The whole church and every believer must be called to prayer.

> Every minister should know that if the prayer meetings are neglected, all his labors are in vain. Unless he can get Christians to attend prayer meetings, all else that he can do will not improve their state of spirituality.[11]

P. T. Forsyth offered an amazing insight,

> But at last, it is truer to say that we live the Christian life in order to pray than that we pray in order to live the Christian life. It is at least as true. Our prayer prepares for our work and sacrifice, but all our work and sacrifice still more prepare for prayer.

Jesus did not only said his house was to be a house of prayer. He said it was to be a house of prayer "for the nations" (Mark 11:17). This approach to prayer moves the church beyond itself to touch the world.

Preaching and Prayer – and Preaching and Prayer

There are different kinds of preaching. When a pastor stands behind a pulpit we may assume that his function is always the same, but actually, it varies. At times, he is:

- An EXHORTER – emphasizing some aspect of established truth, reminding those present of what they already know.
- A TEACHER – unwrapping new ideas from scripture. Expanding their existing knowledge base. Challenging preconceptions. Provoking them to think.
- A PROPHET – warning about the violation of truth, exposing sin patterns and compromise, cold hearts and backsliding, idolatry in its stealth forms and the lack of moral purity. His ultimate beacon is the holiness of God.
- A PREACHER – calling for engagement, on the basis of revealed truth. Preaching asks for a decision; it has an outcome in mind. It provokes to action.
- An EVANGELIST – sharing the gospel and offering the gift of salvation to those who do not know Christ and are following him as disciples. He too calls for a decision, the most basic, will you respond to God's love and be set free from sin, self and Satan?

Pastoral pulpit ministry is at times evangelistic. It exhorts, reminding disciples of truths they already know. It reveals, unwrapping new insights from scripture (teaching). It motivates, moving people to action (preaching). It confronts, refusing to allow compromise to become settled sin (prophet). It invites people to be engaged by God, and to begin the journey of transformation. Prayer moves through all of these phases as well:

- Encouragement through prayer (exhortation) – Jude said that we build ourselves up in prayer (Jude 1:20). That means we pray established truths. Prayer has a goal of self-edification and encouragement, and that happens out of the strength of praying the Word. Pray scripture. Pray truth.
- Insight (teaching) through prayer. Great men often testified that they received more by praying scripture than by its study. The two go hand-in-hand. However, in prayer, this means that you regularly pray unfamiliar passages, new ground. As you pray scripture, new insights

- come. The Holy Spirit teaches you over an open Bible.

- In prayer, you allow the Holy Spirit to search your heart, probing, revealing motives and impurity. Here is the Holy Spirit's gracious judicial role – it is commonly called conviction. It is the nexus of transformation. It is the pathway of repentance and the recalibration of the heart. This is prayer dancing with the prophetic.

- At times, the Holy Spirit in prayer, over an open Bible, will move us to action by declaration (preaching). This is the call of the Spirit, his active direction in our lives – go, stay, stand still, see my salvation. This is alignment with heaven for the purpose of partnership. The Holy Spirit proclaims, announces, declares and asserts, with engagement in view.

- Of course, there are times in prayer where we do the work of pre-evangelism, praying doors to hearts open, blinders off eyes, penetrating regions where people have never heard the gospel, and doing so, first as a prayer evangelist. Prayer must precede evangelism. Evangelism finds its most effective partner in prayer, otherwise, it is intellectual appeal to the gospel. And even if people understand the propositional question, and agree intellectually, it is their heart that must be changed – and that is a work of the Holy Spirit.

There is no effective preaching without prayer, and every aspect of preaching resonates with some aspect of prayer. A pastor comforts and encourages, edifies and exhorts; priestly prayer is designed for the same purpose. A pastor also declares, confronts, motivates to action; prophetic prayer follows a parallel line.

---

1   E.M. Bounds, *The Best of E.M. Bounds* (Baker: Grand Rapids, MI; 1981), 58.
2   Ibid, 61.
3   Ibid, 117.
4   Ibid, 47.
5   Ibid.
6   Ibid.
7   Stephen Olford, *Heart-Cry for Revival* (Westwood, N.J.: Fleming H. Revell, 1962), 68.
8   James Burns, *The Laws of Revival* (Wheaton, IL: World Wide Publications, 1993), 54.
9   P. Douglas Small, *Transforming Your Church into A House of Prayer* (Cleve-

land, TN: Pathway Press, 2006), 57-61.
10   Ibid, 64-68.
11   Charles Finney, "The Purpose of Public Prayer," *The Contemporaries Meet The Classics on Prayer*, ed. Leonard Allen (West Monroe, LA: Howard Publishing, 2003), 206.

CHAPTER 10
Missional Praying

Earlier, we talked about the four critical dimensions in prayer ministry. In those are two big cogs that drive the prayer process. They are rooted in the two great blessings in Scripture – that on the first couple and the home (Gen. 1:28), and the blessing of the Spirit that constituted the Church (Luke 24:50; Acts 2:1-4). These two – at-home and at-church prayer – are the mainsprings of the prayer effort. First, the families of the church gather before God in their homes, for His blessing; and then, the church gathers, not for preaching and teaching, but for prayer.

IDENTIFY INTERCESSORS

The third critical dimension for a healthy, balanced prayer ministry is identified intercessors. Jesus would say *"The harvest is plentiful, but the laborers are few. Therefore pray earnestly…"* (Luke 10:2, ESV). The need is for prayer! Prayer engages the Lord and He 'sends forth laborers.' If anyone is praying at home, daily, it is the intercessors. They are the first people who will show up for church-wide prayer events. The mobilization of intercessors is critical to the success of any prayer effort and to reaching the harvest. But intercessory prayer is not always the best place to begin a prayer ministry. Even intercessors need to learn the value of prayer as communion with God, prayer for the sheer pleasure of God's Presence, prayer that is personally transforming, not only powerfully transactional.

Every believer is called to intercession. And yet, there are those who have a special burden for the role, even a special anointing to do the work of intercession. Most churches have never identified those people. Tragically, intercessors are ignored and often marginalized. Tapping the passion of healthy intercessors will accelerate the prayer effort. Intercessors always have 'prayer fire' in their hearts.

> Intercessory prayer is a petition offered by a believer, before God, the King, on behalf of another. Petition – asking God to do things for us, to grant provision, to direct or protect, is the exclusive 'right' of a believer. Intercession, given such an extraordinary privilege, is the 'responsibility' of a believer. Intercession stands between God and another, and enters a petition on their behalf.

Here are the steps:

1. ***Identify*** the intercessors. Call them together. Spend an evening with them. Appreciate them. Enlist their support. Most of them are eager to be officially engaged as watchers on the wall.

2. ***Train*** them. Don't assume that intercessors naturally do all things perfectly or even understand the workings of prayer. Some intercessors, due to the absence of any training in this area, have a less-than-healthy theology. Teach them. Expose them to balanced prayer theology and practices.

3. ***Team*** them. Many intercessors, like ancient watchmen, tend to be loners, at least in their prayer effort. The 'nightwall' is a lonely place, indeed. Team them, not necessarily to pray together, but to collaborate, to share, to adopt jointly various prayer needs. Create networks of commu-

Missional Praying

> ### Intercessors on Alert
>
> In a small church, a crisis in the life of a member usually calls everyone to prayer. But the larger the church, the more impossible that arrangement becomes. Further, even if intercessors deeply care, if they are bombarded with multiple requests in a day or even in the course of a few days, the exposure to the multiple needs has a numbing effect. The result is that the capacity to empathize is diminished. The larger the church, the more important it is to have a staggered approach to passing on prayer alerts. Use your intercessory teams and rotate them – this request to one Intercessory Prayer Team, and another to a second team, and so forth.
>
> For emergency needs, there should be a contact person to monitor the crisis and pass on new status reports. Use the church website or a facebook group to allow intercessors access to a list, where all the prayer requests are noted, especially prayer alerts. You can even note the team to which a certain need has been assigned. Updates can be quickly obtained from the website if a pastoral care leader or intercessory information coordinator keeps the information fresh. Make sure intercessors have a means of feeding back prayer impressions to those in crisis. But do so through the team process. That provides a check to monitor "words" from the Lord which the Scripture calls us to test. With conference calling so readily available, make it a part of your intercessory ministry. When a major crisis comes, alert intercessors to a phone prayer session at a certain time. Have them pray together by phone. Use Facebook or a Twitter thread for updates.

nication among them. Use teaming to confirm the "impressions" they sense from the Spirit.

4. *Direct* them. If intercessors are "loose cannons," as some pastors allege, it is usually because they have never been directed. Offer them assignments for prayer. Encourage them to adopt ministries of the church for which they will pray. Have every leader and worker enlist intercessors to pray for them regularly.[1]

5. *Debrief* them. If intercessors are the watchers on the wall,

then how do they get their night-watch reports to the elders at the gate? To whom do they report? With whom do they share sensitive impressions? Create a means for intercessors to have input. Seek their insights.

Intercessors should model the spirit of prayer that is desired for the entire church. Don't allow intercessors to become an elite group of super-spiritual types. Healthy intercessors are humble and teachable. They often have a sharp sense of discernment and a deep level of conscientiousness – they want what is right! A servant-spirit restrains those with a healthy prophetic bent. Seasoned intercessors learn to carry deep and often disturbing secrets shared by the Spirit without becoming bitter and caustic. They are often the first to sense a storm coming and the last into the storm shelter out of concern for others. They are often the steadfast silent backbone of a strong and enduring congregation.

A teaming arrangement creates a natural venue for mentoring by veteran intercessors. Don't hesitate to lay down cautions for younger intercessors. Encourage them to let a word from the Lord season before sharing it. Warn them against being a "spiritual bully." Caution them about using "thus saith the Lord" language too casually. Teach them to pray and leave results in the hand of God. It is not the role of the intercessor to enforce either a word or an action. Intercessors, especially those in a prophetic stream, major in truth; remind them that the greater truth is always love. We must "speak truth in love," if truth is to be life-giving. Avoid being judgmental. Don't expect everyone to pray like intercessors. Unite, don't divide. Heal, don't hurt.

Intense fire is used to separate gold from dross. Often, some congregational test will sift intercessors and reveal those with true hearts and noble motives. Trust those who are revealed as mature. Listen to them. Appreciate them. Pastors should pray regularly for and with key intercessors. Teaming allows them to pray for one another, establishing mutual support, creating confirmation and a hedge against isolation and uncertainty. Intercessors come under attack, too. And by the way, when multiple intercessors are experiencing some level of intense warfare, that, too, is a signal for the village that should not be ignored; watchmen are often the first targets in a spiritual raid. Pay attention to intercessors. Gather them for fellowship. Protect them. Dangers for them include cross-gender bonding, power-plays, cliques, divisions, championing single-issue causes, playing the prophet, public posturing, investigative snooping, claiming privileged status for themselves or by connection to another, proxy games ["I speak for so-and-so"], more talk than prayer.

The end effect of intercession is reconciliation. The spiritual warfare is due to resistance from the Evil One who does not desire to see peace with God established in some unbeliever's heart or home. It is a distraction, not the main thing. Persevere, but keep the focus on the connection between God and the subject of prayer. Balance intercession with personal worship. Don't burn out. Don't spend all the time in the closet of intercession.[2] The heart of prayer is communion with God, but the edge of prayer is always mission. Prayer is first God-ward and then outward. A balanced intercessor will not spend all his or her prayer time in intercession. Time must be spent in simply loving the Lord. Further, all prayer is to be wrapped in thanksgiving. Thankful people keep a portal open to God's presence. Healthy intercessors can't live under unrelenting enemy fire. They too must practice the power of praise. Insist on balance in your intercessors. F. B. Meyer asks:

> What has become of so many thousands of our prayers? They were not deficient in earnestness; we uttered them with strong crying and tears. They were not deficient in perseverance; we offered them three times a day for years. They were not deficient in faith; for they have originated in hearts that have never for a moment doubted that God was, and that He

PIT Teams

A PIT crew is a personal intercessory team. Intercession can be a heavy and lonely work. Teaming allows burdens to be shared, impressions to be compared and agreement in prayer to become the common feature of the intercessors work. Consider arranging intercessors into teams of three to five people. The teams don't necessarily meet together for prayer, but the team leader does connect with each member of the PIT crew at least monthly for updates and reports.

In NASCAR country, every driver needs a PIT crew. No race can be won without such a support team. They refuel the car, change the tires, make necessary repairs and get the car back on the track as quickly as possible. Aaron and Hur lifted up the hands of Moses when he was weary. Everyone needs a refueling, renewing team. Consider the need for a PIT crew for every ministry and every ministry leader.

Here is how such a team might function. Following the Moravian principle, "No one works unless someone prays!" Every worker would be encouraged to recruit a primary intercessor. Example: Amelia, a member of 'PIT Crew #1,' has agreed to intercede for April, a Sunday school teacher of juniors. She is the primary intercessor, but every member of 'PIT Crew #1' also adopts April for prayer. Each one of the members also has a primary prayer focus, perhaps more than one. But they each serve to back-up their PIT partners.

In addition to people in the church who need an intercessory team, encourage your teams to adopt people outside the church for prayer: a political leader, a public school teacher or administrator, a policeman or fireman, a doctor or dentist, a nurse or health care provider, a missionary, a nation, an unreached people group, a local gang, notorious and famous unsaved people, a church plant, new families, new Christians, new pastors in the community, a nearby church and the list goes on.

Be careful not to over-commit to prayer. Intercessors do burn out. Formalize your prayer list – with the primary intercessor and his people/projects identified. Then make each intercessor's list available to the entire team. Make a commitment – to pray weekly, as a minimum. PIT crew leaders should have regular contact with the intercessory leader of the church. Reports should flow back-and-forth between intercessors and the individuals for whom they are praying.

was the rewarder of them that diligently sought Him. Still no answer has come...What is the history of these unanswered prayers?...No praying breath is ever spent in vain. If you can believe for the blessings you ask, they are certainly yours. The goods are consigned, though not delivered; the blessing is labeled with your name, but not sent. The vision is yet for an appointed time; it will come and will not tarry. The black head may have become white, the bright eye dim, the loving heart impaired in its beating; but the answer must come at length. God will give the answer at the earliest moment consistent with the true well-being of the one He loves.[3]

Someone observed,

When prayers make long voyages, they come back the richer, loaded with greater treasures. God gives liberal interest for the waiting interval.[4]

4. Prayer Evangelism

The fourth dimension to a local church prayer ministry is prayer evangelism. The energy of prayer needs to be turned outward, toward the community and the world. This is prayer evangelism.

Prayer and Passion

New Testament Christians often see themselves as living in "Acts 29." That is, they believe that the book of Acts is still being written, and the Holy Spirit is still alive and active in and through the Church. With the outpouring of the Spirit, they believe the 'Ghost' of Jesus confirms the Word with signs and wonders in the New Testament era, as well as today. Over the years, something has happened. Passionate praying has virtually disappeared in too many churches. Such prayer marks movements as distinct. Many churches in the first part of the last century were born out of "cottage prayer meetings."

First Corinthians 14 offers wise and practical advice for order in worship. Passionate prayer does not mean disorderly prayer or fleshly aberrations. Passionate prayer does not mean prayer that draws attention to oneself. It does not mean loud or physically demonstrable prayers. Nor does passionate prayer fear the intensity of voices lifted like a holy rumble as they cry out to God corporately. It does not fear tear-stained faces or deep throbs or sighs. It does not fear the searing silence that comes when an entire group is made speechless beneath the *chabod* of God's heavy glory. Some argue that such an intense atmosphere is inappropriate on a Sunday morning with the church full of uninitiated seekers. Sadly, such moments rarely happen in any church-wide setting. Increasingly, even intercessory groups lack passion.

This Age and Passion

Humans are passionate people. We are passionate about sports, hobbies, ecology, vacations, money, work, relationships, stamp-collecting and Civil War memorabilia! But in many churches, emotions are to be checked at the doors of church.

Passion is natural! The Evil One uses passion to his advantage.

Pray Before You Play!

Turn teen "play" events into "prayer" events. Make a deal. Before we go to our party-event, let's take a prayer excursion. Some groups call these Go MAD! outings (Go – Make A Difference!) through prayer, of course. Before you go, call a prayer-huddle. Pray for protection. Pray for direction. Pray that you will leave a deposit of His presence. Stop along the way, as the Lord leads. Pray for schools and churches, pray at city-gateways and seats of power, pray at places of pain and places of promise. And then watch what God might do at the very locations where the group prayed, and with the prayers that were prayed. Then, go have fun. Prayer doesn't have to be segregated from laughter and joy, or from real life. Give thanks. And share with others the Go MAD experiences. Call together a core group at the end of the day and record your impressions. Keep notes of the places visited and the prayers prayed.

We live in a day when "spirit forces of passionate evil have been unleashed upon the earth," so declared psychologist James Stewart, half a century ago. This is not a time for a "milk-and-water passionless theology" or faith, he urged. We will accomplish little by "setting a tepid Christianity against scorching paganism. The thrust of the demonic has to be met with the fire of the divine."[5] New Testament faith with passionate praying is an antidote for the coldness of this hour. Yet, we ourselves are shrinking back, at a time when the atmosphere of our cities is swirling with crosswinds from the middle heaven. Our churches themselves are increasingly the victims of some spiritual stronghold.

> When the presence of Jesus is not manifest in the church in a tangible way and we continue our programs, we are inviting the religious spirit to set up her throne in our congregations and ministries. This spirit is more than happy to become a substitute for Jesus; in fact, it has been the goal of the enemy all along.[6]

"A lack of love for Christ is at the root of all that is wrong with the church today."[7] A loveless church is always a prayerless church. And a praying church is likely to have people who are passionate about Jesus. One pastor sensed that the Spirit was being quenched in his church. He canceled his Sunday night sermon and spoke briefly about his concerns. Then he asked the people to bow their heads and each one who felt he had quenched the Spirit to raise his hand. Nearly every hand went up. That night the service ran late as the people cleared their consciences toward God and one another. Spurgeon observed,

> The condition of the church may be accurately gauged by its prayer meetings. So is the prayer meeting a grace-ometer, and from it we may judge of the amount of divine working among a people. If God be near a church it must pray. And if he be not there, one of the first tokens of his absence will be a slothfulness in prayer.[8]

Dwight Eisenhower rose to fame as a General in World War II. With much attention coming his way, loads of accolades, he responded: "Humility must always be the portion of any man who receives acclaim earned in the blood of his followers and the sacrifices of his friends."[9] We can never claim credit for the stunning victory which came out of the battle of Golgotha. The blood shed there was not our own. In view of his sacrifice, how can we not pray for those who don't know him?

Prayer Evangelism Ideas

Ways to heighten prayer evangelism:

1. Adopt the Moravian principle, "No one works, unless someone prays." Make prayer the essential to every effort. Anything not backed and bathed in prayer is human effort. And human effort along won't result in divine impact. Have every worker recruit a prayer support team. But limit the number on those teams to three to five individuals. Don't allow prayer team recruitment to degenerate into a competition or popularity contest. Everyone should be praying for the pastor, but other teams should be more specific in focus and limited in size.

2. Have church members create a list of family and friends, neighbors and work associates who are not practicing a vital relationship with Christ. Ask them to focus on five names. Challenge them to spend just five minutes day, five days a week praying for those five people. After three months, suggest that they reassess the smaller list in view of the larger list. Give them permission to make alterations. Then do the process over.

3. Celebrate the stories of open hearts, "unpredicted" and divinely orchestrated meetings and unexpected connections, of salvations. Remember, there are no co-incidents! Track the hand of God in response to prayer.

Missional Praying

4. <u>Create a "wailing wall"</u> with the names or pictures of lost loved ones. Keep the fate of souls in front of the congregation.

5. <u>Develop a neighborhood prayer strategy.</u> Emphasize the "prayer-care-share" process.

6. <u>Adopt some territory around your church</u> – a block, ten blocks, a square mile, a definitive subdivision, some specific geographic area. Let that be your mission field. Be good neighbors.

7. <u>Develop a spiritual mapping team.</u> Have them collect data on everything within the determined boundaries. Study crime patterns. Get to know the business owners. Discover potential collaborators, other churches and pastors. Inform key intercessors. Pray for everything that moves in that zone – other churches, businesses, schools, clubs, bars, apartment complexes – everything. Become the change agent in your neighborhood. Put it all on a map. Keep records.

8. <u>Adopt community leaders for prayer.</u> The city-councilperson or commissioner, school board member, etc.

9. <u>Pray for schools and fire houses near your church.</u> Find out if there are special police units assigned to your area. Introduce yourself. Offer to pray for them.

10. <u>Prayer-walk the neighborhood.</u> Not once, but often. Systematically cruise your definitive mission area praying. Watch for changes.

11. <u>Pray over homes for sale</u>! Connect with new neighbors. Be the Welcome Wagon. Don't pressure, just be a good neighbor.

12. <u>Monitor changes in the community</u> – new subdivisions, buildings, new businesses.

13. <u>Do church-wide "care campaigns."</u> Pass out water on a hot day, coffee on a cold day. Set up a prayer tent and give the gift of prayer. Do care projects in the city, but specifically

in your mission zone. Give out food baskets to the needy. Look for creative ways to care – beyond the walls of the church.

14. Evangelism means good news. <u>Make the church a good news institution</u>. Be good news to the poor and the helpless, the hurting and the hopeless, the unloved and the lonely. Be good news in the neighborhood.

15. <u>Send prayer ambassador teams out to nearby businesses</u> with the message, "We're your neighbors at First Church. We wanted to introduce ourselves. We're praying for you." Have them carry a blessing. Jesus called us to be agents of peace in the community.

16. <u>Focus on some high-crime area</u> in your city. Send prayer mission teams into the area to simply pray there. If safe during the day, prayer-walk the area. Look for measurable changes. Don't be surprised if the darkness growls back at you. If it does, don't run; rather, intensify your efforts. Push through; pray through.

17. <u>Pray for the peace of Jerusalem</u>; and pray for some peace-threatening issue in your city, at least monthly.

18. <u>Assign prayer teams to specific areas</u>, businesses, issues. Sponsor on-site prayer gatherings of three to five Christians who meet at a given location once a week for 10 to 15 minutes of prayer. Mark the location of these consistent prayer focus teams on your mission map and gather regular reports from them.

19. Every church needs <u>an identified mission field</u> – one near and one afar. Pick mission fields for which you will regularly pray. Some mission fields are demographic, not geographic. Ask yourself, who can we care for – widows, orphans, single families, the elderly, drug addicts, youth, gangs? Move beyond prayer. Prayer also cares ... and care opens the door for sharing Christ.

20. If your church is in a stable neighborhood, <u>partner with a church in a depressed and socially challenged area</u>. Help

them determine a reasonable target area as a mission field. Stretch your own people beyond their comfort zone. Give the smaller, more challenged church the gift of prayer. Lend intercessory support. Send prayer mission teams. Assist them first with prayer evangelism. Then with care impact strategies. And then equip them to more effectively share the gospel.

The average church has never identified its intercessors. They do the lonely night-watch work without recognition or affirmation. No one wants to hear their watch reports. A church, serious about prayer, must identify and mobilize, direct and affirm intercessors. We do intercede now, but the intercession is largely spent on us, on one another's prayer requests. Intercession and prayer evangelism realign the worshipping church on a horizontal missional axis. That prayer orientation is always secondary, subordinate to the first. The primary alignment is always vertical, always worshipful and transformational. The second discharges the energy of worship on a lost world, loving them open to an encounter with God.

1. P. Douglas Small, *Transforming Your Church into A House of Prayer* (Cleveland, TN: Pathway Press, 2006), 108-130.
2. Small, 123.
3. Quoted by Lockyer, *All the Prayers of the Bible* (Grand Rapids, MI: Zondervan, 1959), 244-245.
4. Lockyer, 245.
5. James Stewart, *A Faith to Proclaim* (Regent College Publishing, 2002), 102-103.
6. Rhonda Hughey, *Desperate for His Presence: God's Design to Transform Your Life and Your City* (Minneapolis, MN: Bethany House, 2004), 79.
7. Clyde Cranford, *Because We Love Him: Embracing a Life of Holiness* (Multnomah Publishing: Sisters, OR; 2002), 112.
8. Jim Cymbala, "Catching Fire," *The Contemporaries Meet The Classics on Prayer,* ed. Leonard Allen (West Monroe, LA: Howard Publishing, 2003), 212.
9. Chuck Swindoll, *So, You Want To Be Like Christ?* (Nashville, TN: W Publishing Group, a division of Thomas Nelson, 2005), 138.

CHAPTER 11
The Strategic Position of Intercession

Intercession is not simply an activity. It is a position; a strategic position. The intercessor takes a position, in the interest of God, with regard to a person, place or thing. The power of prayer here is as much in the strategic position as in any words spoken. *"Except the Lord watch the city, the watchmen watch in vain"* (Psa. 127:1). The power is not in the watchmen - but in God. Yet, God watches in our watching and without our watching, we are left vulnerable, unguarded.

We were created for this post. Adam was placed in the *garden*, but God had the *globe* in mind. His charge was to *grow* and *guard* His garden. The term *'guard,' shamar,* shows up hundreds of times in the Old Testament. It means to watch, keep, guard or preserve. It is a charge to be an 'intercessor' between God and the earth, the garden and the globe, btween things as they were and as they could be. *Shamar* became the 'watchward' of the prophets and even in the New Testament, its equivalent term is used in the repeated call to 'watch' and pray, to be vigilant. In the failure of Adam to 'watch,' to guard, to protect, Satan gained an advantage and Adam lost the strategic high ground of the garden, which had offered the tree of life.

Jesus, the last Adam, has legally recovered the strategic middle which the first Adam forfeited. This embattled turf is what Jesus came to the earth to reclaim. It is, however, what Lucifer stubbornly and illegitimately continues to purport to own. Intercession is always in the strategic middle, between God and disconnected men and women, disconnected peoples and places.

The dominion granted to Adam at Creation when he was placed in the middle, between God the Creator and all of Creation, has now been reclaimed. Jesus declared, *"All authority is given to me in heaven and earth,"* (Mt. 28:18), *"therefore go..."* We do not presumptuously aspire to this role.

God puts us all in some garden – a family, a church, a neighborhood or a city, a company or a circle of friends. Our role is to 'grow it,' to cultivate relationships and spiritual potential; and also, to 'guard' it, serving as a spiritual watchman. That also means serving as a spiritual mediator. Sometimes, that is in the posture of a priestly advocate, praying for another as if we were the person. At times, it is in the posture of a prophet, praying for the in-breaking hand of God to enforce His will.

INTERCESSION: THE UNCOMFORTABLE MIDDLE

In Luke 11:1, the disciples, after hearing Jesus pray, asked, *"Teach us to pray!"* Robert Murray McCheyne said, "If I could hear Jesus praying for me in the next room, I should not fear a thousand devils."[1] What follows the familiar Lord's Prayer in Luke 11 is a parable. There are three players in the story. One is a traveler who comes into a city after dark. Without housing or food, he remembers that a friend lives there. He locates him and knocks on

> **From the Diary of David Brainerd**
>
> Had little life and power in the forenoon: near the middle of the afternoon God enabled me to wrestle ardently in intercession for absent friends: but just at night the Lord visited me marvelously in prayer. I think my soul never was in such an agony before. I felt no restraint, for the treasures of divine grace were opened to me. I wrestled for absent friends, for the ingathering of souls, for multitudes of poor souls, and for many that I thought were the children of God in many distant places. I was in such an agony, for half an hour before sunset, till near dark, that I was all over wet with sweat: but yet it seemed to me that I had wasted away the day, and had done nothing. Oh!, my dear Savior did sweat blood for poor souls! I longed for more compassion toward them. Felt still in a sweet frame, under a sense of divine love and 'Farewell, vain world; my soul can bid Adieu. My Savior taught me to abandon you. Your charms may gratify a sensual mind. But cannot please a soul for God Designed.'
>
> – David Brainerd

his door. He is welcomed warmly. But there is a problem. While his host can provide housing for the night, he apparently recognizes hunger in the eyes of his traveling friend, but he has no bread in the house. The urgent need demands immediate attention and cannot wait until tomorrow. And yet, the time is midnight. Even Walmart is closed.

Alas, the host has another friend who always has plenty. He goes to that endowed friend and insists he rise from his bed, answer the door and lend him bread. This well-supplied friend with plenty is the most resistant. The story is designed to emphasize our need for persistence in prayer. Will the friend in the uncomfortable middle be denied? Does he have a strong enough relationship with the friend with plenty to sustain such an intrusion at midnight? Will he give up and let his friend in need go hungry?

The friend in the middle will not be denied. He is as intense as if he were the hungry one. This is the true spirit of intercession.

We pray as if we are the person we are representing in prayer. Their need becomes, by empathy and the assignment of the Spirit, our need. Intercession places us in the uncomfortable middle. All of us have unsaved friends. Sometimes they call at midnight, and a call after midnight is rarely a good call. They turn to us in crisis looking for support in the time of a personal storm.

God knows, in placing us in the middle, that we can't meet their need. The middle position demands humility. Many people shrink back from the middle and deliver their needy friends to a Christian professional – "Here, you are trained. Deal with this. Help them." But God wants every believer in the middle. We pray, and He does the miracles. We make the introductions; and He reveals Himself as alive.

> There is a mighty lot of difference between saying prayers and praying.
> – John G. Lake

We prefer the end! That is, we want to be on the end of the blessing, with someone more spiritual in the middle. So much of American Christianity is about receiving – receiving a blessing or breakthrough from the Lord. But the greater blessing is never on the end. It is the blessing that comes from being in the middle.

Intercession: The Need for Persistence

In the parable, the friend with plenty is at first resistant. The design of the story is intended to emphasize the need for persistence. And having made that initial point, Jesus sweetens the dynamic, *"If a son asks bread of any of you that is a father..."* (Luke 11:11) A son? A father? No longer are we a friend going to a resistant friend with plenty. We are sons, going to the father with plenty who is never reticent to answer. Luther said, "We pray for silver, but God often gives us gold instead."[2]

We give up too easily. *"If you...know how to give good gifts to your children how much more shall your heavenly father give the Holy Spirit to them that ask him?"* (Luke 11:13) I love the "how much more!" of this passage. "Ask, seek, knock" – and you will receive, and you will find, and doors will be opened. All three terms are in the present tense. *Keep on* asking until you get an answer. *Keep on* seeking until you make a discovery that leads to a breakthrough. *Keep on* knocking until you disturb heaven and God opens some doorway.

Not only are these terms in the *present tense,* they are in the *imperative mood.* Ask with intensity. Seek relentlessly. Knock forcefully. This is not sissy praying. Not your typical prayer meeting. This is vigorous prayer. These are weighty expressions of hunger and need. They are compelling pleas, animated yearnings, driving prayers, urgent appeals. They are reasoned, but throbbing petitions.

Our prayers lack such intensity. The result is that our words *say* that we are desperate for God, for friends and family to know him, for a Great Awakening in our culture. But our *lack of persistence* and our less than intense mood reveals that we are willing to live without the requests we say we so desperately seek. Without persistent, imperative praying, our unsaved friends will remain lost. If we are not praying for them, who is?

Intercession: The Problem of Interference

In intercession, the middle position, we grasp the hand of God to touch the world through prayer. That upward grasp is the greater and more strategic grasp. Like reaching over a cliff for someone below, the task is daunting, and it can become a dark experience if the upward tether is not firm. Intercessors who do not keep their prayer lives centered in the simplicity of communion with God endanger both themselves and their mission. It is the necessary peace in the midst of every intercessory storm. It is not uncommon in such moments to have simultaneously a holy and unholy encounter; to experience peace *and* a sense of conflict; to see victory and defeat *together*. This clash of light and darkness is the influence of both heaven and hell on our world. An intercessor steps into a vortex of such swirling powers. Sometimes it is like being on the edge of a thunder cell. Explosive and stormy discharges of disruptive energy are possible. This demands that we pray with an awareness of the schemes of the Evil One. Though prayer is focused Godward, it often gains the attention of the Evil One. Flashes of warfare are not uncommon before, after and during seasons of intercession. We cannot allow ourselves to be conditioned into avoidance of intercession to escape such warfare moments. Prayer is just for such moments.

Intercession: The Position of a Watchman

In ancient times, a city could perish due to the negligence of a watchman. He served as an obstacle to an intruder, and was the first wave of defense. The city could sleep because he was awake. So critical was the watchman's role, that caught sleeping, death might be the penalty. If danger threatened, he was to sound an alarm. The Scripture warns that we are to be aware [the implied role of the watchman, and therefore of prayer] of the *"devil's schemes"* (2 Corinthians 2:11; see also Ephesians 6:10-18). Watchmen were to be ever "alert," a term used to describe a sentry – the watchman were posted on the wall or at the gate of city.

Prayer itself is an alert system that heightens awareness of some coming storm or prepares us for it. Nothing takes God by surprise. Because prayer's warning system nurtures obedience and assures our hearts of certain triumph, as a result, there are few things Satan hates more. The book *The Kneeling Christian* reminds us, "Satan laughs at our toilings and mocks our wisdom, but he trembles when we pray." It is not our power in prayer, but the invitation for God's mighty hand to enter the fray, a power with which Lucifer cannot contend. There is nothing the devil dreads so much as prayer!

There is much emphasis today on spiritual warfare, but the goal of intercession is not spiritual warfare. Rather, it is reconciliation. The focus of intercession in some circles has degenerated to warfare tirades against the darkness. God has not called us to warfare. It is an ancillary, often unavoidable, but not central. The Scriptures say, *"Wisdom is better than warfare"* (Ecclesiastes 9:18). When an intercessor steps into the critical, uncomfortable middle,

---

Watchmen on the Wall

Intercession has often been likened to the role of the watchman. The ideal is to have watchmen on the wall 24 hours a day, 7 days a week. Few churches can achieve that goal. But in special seasons, as a church moves toward such a noble goal, you can recruit people to pray in 30-minute segments and cover the 168 hours in a week. As one intercessor completes his prayer time, he calls the next person on the list. If he doesn't get an answer, he is not relieved. So have back-ups ready to fill in for no-shows. Keep a watchman on the wall! Let the prayer chain not be broken. Provide guides for people to use in the 30-minute watches. Open the church during this season, at least during the day. Some might prefer to come there.

If your week of prayer is successful, consider expanding it to two weeks, or even a month. When you solicit recruits, make the timeline of the commitment clear. Create a place on-line for regular updates – a blog or a message board attached to your church web-site. Have each person note their experience as if they were entering a report into a collective group journal. Reading the reports should be an encouragement. During the week of prayer, ask everyone to "pray without ceasing." Pray for the watchman on the wall anytime you see a clock or think about the ongoing prayer effort.

warfare is inevitable. That place is occupied illegally by Satan in his attempt to separate man from God. But the inevitable spiritual conflict cannot be the primary focus of the intercessor. His role is to connect the lost or displaced person to God, and God through prayer, to that person.

The goal of intercession is reconciliation. The work of the Evil One is to distract, to cause us to miss our purpose. He creates confusion among intercessors regarding their role in the middle, or he attempts to displace them completely. We must stay in the middle, sometimes battling very real distractions, even intense personal interferences, and yet making our prayers of reconciliation the main thing. We pray holding the tools of edification in one hand and the sword in the other (Neh. 4:15-17). We don't want to fight. We are not called primarily to fight; we are called to build up, to edify, to strengthen, to intercede from our place on the wall.

> Preaching affects time; prayer affects eternity.
> - Leonard Ravenhill

Children as Intercessors

In an old YMCA type building in Argentina there were about 50 children, ranging in age from four or five to their teens. They led worship, shared testimonies, and ministered to the international guests. Following the formal service, the children moved through the audience to pray for those in attendance. A six-year-old boy told how a girl had stolen his lunch money. He prayed for her, and the next day she brought his money back and apologized. Then he led her to Jesus! Unbelievable! These children turned toward the audience. They didn't just go systematically. They looked, and they waited for instructions from the Lord. Then they went to specific people to pray for them. The prayers were simple, yet powerful. Many of them simply praised God, saying repeatedly, "Recibelo, recibelo! Receive it, receive it."

All over the earth, children are being raised up as intercessors. It is an unprecedented and unbelievable phenomenon. The Children's Global Prayer Movement brochure features some of their comments:

- ♦ "I'm a world-class intercessor now." – Aaron, 11.
- ♦ "My awesome prayer power works!" – Tom, 6.
- ♦ "I'm not just cute, I'm a mighty prayer warrior. Thank you." – Breanna, 4.
- ♦ "My desire to pray isn't strange. It's from God!" – Jenna, 8.
- ♦ "Praying is more fun than toys." – Jesse, 5.
- ♦ It's time to pray not play, weep not sleep." – Kelly, 9.

Esther Ilinsky of the child intercessor movement says, "A new breed of children – righteous seed – has emerged on the world scene. These are world class intercessors – World Shapers...They are praying for their peers, the two billion children age twelve and under who live on earth" that they might know Christ.

Peter, quoting Joel, declared, *"Your sons and daughters [the children] shall prophesy"* (Acts 2:17). The promise, Peter declared, is *"for your children!"* Tragically, we have offered the entertainment of children's church rather than introduction to life in the Spirit. When Jesus rode into Jerusalem, the children cried out, *"Hosanna to the Son of David"* (Matthew 21:8). Religious leaders objected then, as now, to such religious fervor from children. Jesus said, *"Out of the mouth of infants and nursing babes you have perfected [prepared] praise!"* Jesus is saying again, *"Permit the children to come to me!"* Corporate prayer should never be a childless event. God wants intergenerational prayer. Children can teach us so much about simple faith and earnest prayer.

Fifteen Subjective Identifiers of Intercessors

1. At times, you feel <u>a compelling call to break away for prayer</u> – to get alone with God for some reason, and pray, even in the middle of the day.
2. You have experienced <u>a 'burden' to pray</u>, like an inner grip on your soul and consciousness, that will not go away. It may ebb and flow for days, abating and then coming on you like the rising tide – you must pray.
3. You sense <u>passion and compassion</u> when you pray. You find yourself praying with your heart as much or more than your head.
4. <u>Tears are common</u>, though no one may have taught you the role of 'lament' in prayer, and you may be unaware of the huge number of psalms that fit that category. You weep. You travail. Your tears become prayers in and of themselves. You can't turn them off – even after you have left your prayer closet.
5. <u>You experience impressions, vague right-brain thoughts, intuitive hunches</u>, the outline of which is sometimes imprecise and ambiguous. You are compelled to pray, but unsure about what and how to pray – you feel caught between knowing and not fully knowing, as if you have walked into some conversation, some scene without context. Even time and place seem indeterminate.
6. <u>You are frequently awakened in the night</u> – and called to pray. The Biblical term is the 'watch.' You may sit for hours in a prayerful attitude with no leading to say a word, no clue of why God awakened you, no sense of your prayer mission. Spiritually, you are in some watch-tower, on some wall, between inside and outside, light and dark, the saved and the lost, at times between the Evil One and some struggling soul. Just your prayerful presence on the wall makes the mysterious difference in some matter.
7. <u>People come before you in your mind for prayer</u> – and you feel obligated to stop, to pray for them, as if some danger is imminent or some opportunity might be missed, if you did not do so.
8. <u>You may have a dream or open vision of someone</u> or of a place (you have never been there or it might be familiar to you). You are drawn to pray for the place or the people there. Perhaps, a specific person, at times, a face or form is presented to you for prayer, by the Holy Spirit. At such times you pray by faith. You must, since the subject of your prayer is more familiar to you in the realm of the Spirit, than the natural.
9. <u>You are caught up</u>, at times, <u>into a spirit of prayer</u>. You pray beyond yourself. You know what it is like to be 'anointed' to pray, to lose track of time in prayer.

Intercession and Spiritual Power

In 1871, D. L. Moody's Chicago church burned and the next year, while it was being rebuilt, he visited England to raise funds, listen to and learn from England's great preachers. One Sunday he agreed to minister at a church in London. The experience was a disaster. Moody said he had never had such a difficult time preaching in his life. A deadness seem to grip the service. Relieved that the service was over, he realized that he had to preach there again that night.

That evening, however, the atmosphere was different. The church was packed and there was an air of expectancy. Moody said, "The powers of an unseen world seemed to have fallen upon the audience." At the end of his message, he gave an invitation for people to acknowledge Christ as Lord. He was astounded when 500 people stood, thinking they had misunderstood he demanded that everyone be seated. He repeated the invitation, and again 500 people stood. Still confused, he again attempted to separate out the insincere. But all 500 went to the vestry to pray to receive Christ. Night after night, he continued to preach an unscheduled meeting. A revival had started in a cold church. What had effected the change? Moody knew it was not his preaching alone.

One woman left the service that Sunday morning and casually told her invalid sister that a visitor named Moody had preached that morning. The invalid sister became ashen. "Mr. Moody from Chicago?" she inquired with surprise. The invalid sister had read about Moody and had been secretly praying for God to send him to London to preach in that very church. "If I had known he was going to preach this morning, I would have eaten no breakfast and spent the whole time he was preaching in prayer for him. Now, sister, go out of the room, lock the door, send me no dinner; no matter who comes, don't let them see me. I am going to spend the

10. <u>You pray in the Spirit</u> – with groans, sounds not discernible. You feel compelled to give voice to some deep spiritual sensation, as if travailing in birth, the struggle being within you, but you have no language for it – you groan, you weep and lament.
11. <u>You imagine yourself at times in places far away</u>, yet, it is as if you are <u>here and there at the same time</u>, space knowing no limits. At other times, it is as if, on some magic carpet of prayer, you are whisked away. On some occasions, you may feel that you have been with some missionary in a desperate lonely place. Then, as if you have crawled into a dungeon to sit with someone in solitary confinement. You may sense yourself praying desperately, kneeling by some missionary who you know to be on the other side of the world; somehow, you have joined your voice to their voice in prayer. You may feel that you are before royalty – pleading for some righteous cause.
12. <u>God has whispered to you a secret</u>, perhaps, more than one – and you have prayed about His disclosures, and kept His secret.
13. God's secrets are not always delightful disclosures. At times, by the Spirit, you see through a person, God revealing their heart to you – this is the prophetic dimension of intercession. <u>At times</u> it places <u>you in a terribly uncomfortable situation</u> of disclosing to a pastor or elder what <u>you know, but only know in the spirit</u>. You are a watcher on the wall, not an elder at the gate – release the report of what you saw, what you sense, no more and no less, and trust leaders. God will confirm your disclosure – don't go rogue, don't enforce a conviction. Stay in your office.
14. Priestly intercessors sometimes <u>feel the pain of others</u>; they bear the burden of another in prayer. These are often called 'sympathy' pains. They are clues for prayer and motivators for passionate prayer. Be careful! Christ himself has borne our griefs and sorrows, and was afflicted with our sickness. We take such matters, in prayer, to the cross, and in doing so, we may momentarily taste pain and hurt, but the burden must be borne by cross. Witches and sorcerers take on the sickness of others in their cure of them, that is a line you dare not violate. Feel the burden, sense the grief, carry the person to the cross in prayer.
15. At times, intimacy with God has placed in you some vision, some promise, and you have learned the necessity of carrying the seed to term, not miscarrying, but eventually giving birth, in prayer, to some noble purpose of God. Remember, intimacy produces the child, but travail delivers it; and there can never be a birth, first, without intimacy. Balance <u>prayer between intimacy and intercession</u>.

The Strategic Position of Intercession

> You may not have a developed sense of such clear visions described above. You may not understand the international missional impact of an intercessor. In fact, these ideas may seem strange to you, and then again, they may be like an opaque windowpane through which you have occasionally stared, Paul's dark glass (1 Cor. 13:12). Such spirit-journeys are best kept secret; between you and the Holy Spirit. Pride longs to sensationalize. Humility conceals honor. Heaven will reward it.

whole afternoon and evening in prayer!"

Paul engaged the Thessalonians to serve as an intercessory support team. *"Pray,"* he said, *"that the Word of the Lord may have free course..."* (2 Thess. 3:1). The idea is that prayer spreads the speed of the gospel – and aids in its full cultural impact. It triumphs. Through the principles of Scripture are powerful the seeds must be carried on the wind of the Spirit. The Spirit comes by prayer; and accompanies the Word as it goes forth.

Moody had stood in the pulpit that morning alone without intercessory support. He had the words; he preached from Scripture. But that night, the ice chamber he had experienced in the morning met fire. Hard hearts were now hungry and tender. The Word of God ran into hearts without the interference of indifference? And that was because of the prayers of a bedridden saint who was interceding. Moody heard about the woman and recruited her as an intercessor for the rest of her life.[3]

---

1   Lockyer, *All the Prayers of the Bible* (Grand Rapids, MI: Zondervan, 1959), 221.
2   Ole Kristian Hallesby, *Prayer*, 104
3   E. M. Bounds. *The Classic Collection on Prayer* (Bridge-Logos Publishers: Gainesville, FL; 2001), 571-572.

CHAPTER 12
Prayer Evangelism – The Extension of God's Love

The late Dr. Ray H. Hughes is a legend in Pentecostal circles. He was the President of Lee University and subsequently, the denomination's School of Theology. He was General Overseer of the Church of God three times, president of the National Association of Evangelicals and chairman of three Pentecostal World Conferences. He represented the Pentecostal movement to Presidents Reagan, Carter and George H. W. Bush, often in meetings in which Billy Graham represented Evangelicalism.

But he may have never been saved apart from intercession. He often told the story of the afternoon he ran home from school and dashed through the front door. Picking up his ball glove and heading out the back door, he heard a captivating sound from upstairs. Drawn to the music of prayer, he slowly climbed the steps. The sounds became clear words. The voice was that of his mother. She was pleading with God, *"Save my boy Ray!"*

Like something driven deep into the heart, Ray Hughes never

escaped that moment. Like a deer who continues to run a short distance after the battle with the hunter is over, his running from God was near its end. The intercessory spirit that makes prayer a merciful net had captured him. The arrow of God's love expressed in his mother's voice had gone deep into his heart. God would not let him go. Prayer harnessed him, and God, through him, touched a world.

Prayer Evangelism

The apostle Paul urged entreaties and prayers *"on behalf of all man for kings and all who are in authority"* because God *"desires all men to be saved and to come to the knowledge of truth"* (cf. 1 Tim. 2:1-3, NASB).

He expressed a desire for prayer to be proliferated *"in every place,"* with men *"lifting holy hands,"* the posture of blessing (v. 8). The apostle suggested the outcome of such prayer would lead to *"peaceful and quiet lives marked by godliness and dignity."* Prayer then, changes us. It sharpens our witness. But Paul is also suggesting that it impacts the city in which we live. It affects leaders and the unsaved. It is the key to evangelism and awakening.

The *highest calling* of prayer is communion with God. But the *noblest use* of prayer is as an intercessor, especially when we pray for the lost. Sometimes we can't pray for ourselves. That's when we need an intercessor. Sensitivity in prayer will never allow us to focus only on our own needs. Praying for those under stress and pressure around us is so important. Hold up the hands of Christian leaders through prayer. Ultimately, the great role of intercession is not representing others before God, but advocating for God in behalf of others. It isn't capturing the pain on the earth, but the pain in God's heart for the earth. We must move from asking God to take care of the things that are breaking our hearts, to praying about the things that are breaking His heart.[1]

The Gift of Prayer

In a culture that is increasingly resistant to the gospel, prayer may be the greatest avenue to make them aware of God's gracious love. Give the gift of prayer to the unsaved. Dr. Al Vander Griend offered the story of a store owner in New York. A pastor occasionally shopped there.

As far as the pastor knew, the store owner was not a Christian. His location was in a high crime area, not the safest or most desirable spot. One day he called the pastor in a rather frantic mood. "My store keeps getting robbed, and there are drug dealers in front of my place day and night. Pastor, what are you going to do about it?" Pastor Alex asked, "Why don't you call the police?" The shopkeeper confessed that he had called the police and they had told him there was nothing that could be done about the situation. "So," he said, "I am calling you."

In a nation increasingly out of control, our only hope is the intervention of God. But the church is largely unprepared to respond. At first the pastor was baffled, but then God reminded him of the powerful impact of on-site prayer. "I'll tell you what. Let me come down to your store once a week with a group, and we will pray that God will intervene. Is that okay?" The storeowner agreed.

That Thursday afternoon, shoppers heard a strange sound coming from the backroom of the store. In the subsequent weeks,

> **Prayer Ambassadors**
>
> Much of the current emphasis on intercession has bent it to the prophetic side. But intercession is as much about being a priest. Priestly intercessors unite. They heal divisions. They work toward reconciliation. They speak peace. They are ambassadors of grace. Send teams of "prayer ambassadors" out to speak peace over the community. Start with businesses that are owned by members of the church. Pray for the neighborhood around the church.

> **For Whom Should We Intercede?**
> ♦ **Enemies** – Luke 6:28; Matthew 5:44
> ♦ **God's people** – 1 Samuel 22:23
> ♦ **Friends** – James 5:16
> ♦ **Family** – 2 Samuel 7:17
> ♦ **Fellowmen** – 1 Timothy 2:1
> ♦ **Fellow workers in Christ** – 2 Thessalonians 3:1
> ♦ **Fellow members in the church** – Ephesians 6:18
> ♦ **Kings and all in authority** – 1 Timothy 2:1-4
> ♦ **For the land** – 2 Samuel 21:14
> ♦ **For the lost** – Romans 10:1
> ♦ **For nations** – Ezekiel 22:30; Isaiah 56:7; Mark 11:17
> ♦ **For preachers of the Gospel** – Colossians 4:2; 2 Thessalonians 3:1
> ♦ **For those over us** – 1 Kings 13:6; Ezra 6:10
> ♦ **Jerusalem** – Psalm 122:6

some asked the store owner what was happening "back there!" Pastor Alex recalls, "We prayed in earnest that God would protect the store and the drug dealers would be dealt with."

Within four weeks, four drug dealers were arrested. Two families who shopped at the neighborhood store began to attend Pastor Alex's church. The store owner saw the hand of God. Prayer should never be a thing we keep to ourselves. Intercession is a gift. We use our relationship with God for the good of others. And God, who desires to touch through us, begins to do just that.

The Three "Greats" of the New Testament

Sadly, only nine percent of adults can correctly identify the term, *the Great Commission,* as the last command of Christ to tell his story to the world. Eighty-four percent did not even have a clue as to what the term meant.[2] *"Go into all the world and preach the gospel to every creature;" "Go ye therefore and teach all nations..."*

(Mark 16:15; Matthew 28:19). A paraphrase could be understood in this way, "As you are going about in the earth proclaim Christ; wherever you are, share Jesus. Tell the story of His good news and His love!" All of us are called to do that.

The *Great Commission* needs to be wrapped in the *Great Commandment* to have maximum impact. The Great Commandment is: *"You shall love the Lord your God with all your heart"* (Matthew 22:37-39). Loving God with all our heart, our mind and might, until the power and effect of that love transforms our love for our neighbor, and we love others as we love our self. That is the message of the Great Commandment.

Something happens in conversations with people who feel that we love them. Love changes the relational environment. Love breaks down resistance. Love is irresistible. Truth without love is like bitter medicine without sugar. Truth is the fact of the gospel; love is reality of the gospel. Truth is the head talking; love is the heart touching. Truth is propositional; love is incarnational. The Commission and the Commandment have to go together.

Paul gave us another "great." It is sometimes called the *Great Commitment*:

> I exhort first of all that supplications, prayers, intercessions and the giving of thanks be made for all men, for and all who are in authority...this is good...in the sight of God our Savior who desires all men to be saved and to come to the knowledge of the truth (1 Timothy 2:1-4).

Prayer aimed at community leaders and the unsaved is the key to getting them into a relationship with God. It is also the key to a safe community, according to Paul.

- In Colossians 4:3, Paul suggests that *"prayer opens doors."*
- In 2 Corinthians 4:4, he indicates that the *"god of this world"* blinds the minds of those who believe not. Non-believers need prayer to heighten spiritual perception before

they can believe. It is not the head we are after, not alone; it is the heart. So prayer precedes the appeal. It reaches inside and touches a hard heart. It opens closed and blinded eyes.

- *"Open my eyes, that I may behold wondrous things out of your law* [Word]," the psalmist declares (Psalm 119:11).

Intercession is the means by which we pray the blinders off unbelievers. And communion with God, the basis for intercession, the context of it, is the means by which we ourselves are changed into credible witnesses. The more we pray for the unsaved around us, the more we find God loving them through us. Prayer changes us, and it works to open the hearts of our friends to the reality of God's presence. And sensing God's love, those previously closed to the gospel and the reality of God, are suddenly open to consider truth. The Great Commitment, prayer, empowers us to love at the level of the Great Commandment. And the Great Commandment, love, driven by the power of the Great Commitment, prayer, paves the way for the Great Commission, the effective sharing of the gospel. "Prayer Evangelism" is the root of all successful evangelism.

INTERCESSION AND THE LOST

The Great Commission is not optional; it is a command. Love infects us. We have to talk about Christ. He saved us; we cannot help but whisper His name. To see the world dying and withholding life-giving support is criminal. How can we keep quiet? Prayer strengthens us for that task. And prayer opens the hearts of those for whom we are praying. Prayer, in fact, creates the connection that allows the sharing of faith to take place.

Intercession is the call to stand between God and the lost! Along with scripture, it is the greatest tool that we have been given for the task of completing the Great Commission. Yet, Barna notes that:

Privatized faith is common in contemporary America because it is so very congenial with a highly differentiated society. Restricted largely to spheres of family and personal life, it encroaches very little into the public world, which Americans increasingly define as off-limits to religion.[3]

At a prayer summit, with pastors of different denominations from across a city, I recall a pastor praying, "I thank you God for Rachelle Wilson. I remember the morning I went to work, pushed my time card into the clock, turned to Rachelle and said, 'I have something to tell you.' She looked at me and said, 'You got saved this weekend. Now I can check you off my list.'"

Rachelle was a Christian, but she was more. She was an intercessor, a woman of prayer. She had found a way to combine work and ministry. She kept the time clock for the company. As a result, she had the task of regularly reviewing all the names of the workers at her company. Without any fanfare, as she regularly reviewed the names, Rachelle prayed for the salvation of every worker. She called their names out to God silently. She asked God to save them and change their lives.

Almost immediately, after that pastor finished, another pastor prayed. "God, I, too, want to thank you for Rachelle Wilson..." Both men, as sinners, had worked at the same company in different

> **Prayers to Fulfill the Great Commission**
> ♦ **Acts 1:14-15** – The church assembled for prayer as they waited for the Spirit to come and give them power to be witnesses to Christ in all the world.
> ♦ **Acts 4:23-35** – The growing church met the threat of persecution with prayer that resulted in renewed grace and power.
> ♦ **Acts 10:1-47** – Cornelius and Peter were brought together as each of them prayed. Then the door of faith was opened to the Gentiles.
> ♦ **Acts 13:1-4** – The powerful world missionary ministry of Paul grew out of a prayer meeting to minister to the Lord.

> **Praying for Non-Believers**
> **ASK GOD...**
>
> 1. To send believers into their lives as a witness (Matthew 9:38).
> 2. To open their spiritual eyes and that Satan will not blind them from the truth (2 Corinthians 4:4).
> 3. To give them ears to hear (Matthew 13:15), faith to believe (Acts 20:21), the will to respond (Acts 16:14; Romans 10:9).
> 4. To help them understand and believe the Scriptures (Luke 24:45; Romans 10:17; 1 Thessalonians 2:13).
> 5. To draw them to himself (John 6:44).
> 6. For the Holy Spirit's conviction of their sin and that he will guide them into all truth (John 16:8-11).
> 7. That He will grant them the grace of true repentance and saving faith (Acts 3:19; Ephesians 2:8-9).
> 8. To increase their desire to know Him (2 Chronicles 15:4; Acts 17:27).
> 9. That they will believe in Christ as Savior (John 1:12; John 5:24; Acts 16:31) and submit to Him as Lord (Romans 10:9-10).
> 10. That they surrender everything to follow Christ (Matthew 16:24; 2 Corinthians 5:15; Philippians 3:7-8).
> 11. To set them free from spiritual captivity (2 Timothy 2:25-26).
> 12. That they grow in the grace and knowledge of Christ (2 Peter 3:18).
> 13. That they continue to live in Christ (Colossians 2:6-7).
> 14. To sanctify them, not only from the world and sin, but unto himself for a holy purpose and mission (Romans 12:1-2).
> 15. To give them opportunities to witness (Colossians 4:3), as young believers (Acts 2); for boldness in witness (Acts 4:29).

years. They had never met before but in the context of this prayer event, they discovered not only their common work background, but their common connection with a faithful woman of prayer who had wrestled for their souls. Now, both were in ministry serving churches of different denominations in the same city because of this one faithful workplace intercessor.

Intercession: God Loving Through Us in Prayer

Love constrains. And prayer lengthens the arms of love, reaching beyond our human capacity. Paul declared,

> Since the day we heard of you, we have not stopped praying for you and asking God to fill you with the knowledge of his will through all spiritual wisdom and understanding. And we pray this in order that you may live a life worthy of the Lord and may please him in every way, bearing fruit...growing... being strengthened (Colossians 1:9-11, NIV).

Susan Gaddis says, the "intercessor is an advocate, one who represents or pleads the cause of another."[4] William Law notes, "Nothing makes us love someone so much as praying for them."[5] Luther called prayer, "climbing into the heart of God."

There is perhaps no greater way to impact a person's life than to consistently pray for them. Leonard Ravenhill declares, "To stand before men on behalf of God is one thing, to stand before God on behalf of men is something entirely different." Andrew Murray says,

> Time spent in prayer will yield more than that given to work. Prayer alone gives work its worth and its success. Prayer opens the way for God Himself to do His work in us and through us. Let our chief work as God's messengers be intercession; in it we secure the presence and power of God to go with us.[6]

This is the premier role of the intercessor. Stepping into a gap and standing before the Lord! There the intercessor stands in behalf of the other party – perhaps someone in great need; or someone without a relationship with the Lord; or someplace deserving of and about to receive discipline. At times, with a sense of urgency, the intercessor races to stand between God and some offending party (Numbers 16:47-48).

And by that act, intercession calls a truce. It pleads for mercy. It builds a protective wall around the one who is guilty! It doesn't remove the offense; but it may delay judgment. This is not a hostile act against God or a defiant position taken that resists either his right to discipline or the need for it. The intercessor is strangely acting in behalf of God, indeed, with God. The act is not only justified by God, but orchestrated by His Spirit; indeed, it was emulated by Jesus. It seeks to protect the guilty from God in His necessary role as Judge, and in behalf of His role as Father and Creator. It provides a momentary reprise from wrath or punitive action that is admittedly deserved (1 Samuel 2:25)! And more so, from the ambush of the Evil One whose role is to steal and kill, who also acts a prosecutor, a kind of Rambo bounty-hunter, an accuser of 'the brethren' and destroyer of those in darkness. He is no friend to those who have entered a covenant with him by sin.

Stepping into this gap is precisely what God wants us to do.[7] While intercession does not remove either the record of the sin or its effect, nor eliminate due compensation for sin, it does create time and space for the Holy Spirit to work. Intercession, partnering with the Holy Spirit, calls the individual to repent. It longs for godly disposition and godward direction to emerge. It pleads for open eyes, for the hold of bondage of sin and Satan to be broken. It pulls victims *"out of the fire"* (Jude 1:23). Oh the power of intercession.

The *delight* of prayer is found in our communion with God. The *duty* of prayer, though not without delight, but driven by a sense of mission, is found in intercession. You cannot intercede with balance until and unless you spend time in communion. Communion with God is the cause behind intercession. Having experienced the rest and peace of God (communion), we project that very rest and peace toward people and places where it is absent. We invite the

Prince of Peace to assert His rule in that troubled heart or home, that neighborhood or nation. The soul that is saved is first claimed by prayer. Wherever the Spirit brings liberty to a life, invariably, an intercessor has tracked through the rubble declaring by prayer the power of God's grace in that person or place.[9]

Intercession and the Character of God

The very fact that we pray to God is an indication of our faith, not only in God's *ability*, but in His *character*. The child who screams for parental assistance doesn't analyze the parent's capacity to respond to the situation. The cry is an appeal to their compassion.

> **Kneeling in Prayer**
>
> Prayer is an activity that involves the whole person. If in our communication with God we thwart and exclude part of ourselves, the neglected side of our person will still be present as a saboteur and protester, preventing prayer from really "taking off" or going deep. If we try to leave behind our mind...the mind, suddenly starved, will dredge up all manner of inconsequential garbage...silence and stillness is invaded...If we neglect our hearts...by confining our prayer to thinking religious thoughts and intellectualizing about God, prayer remains dry...[9]
>
> It is the disallowance of the body in prayer that may hurt prayer most. In the last few decades, Christians have been kneeling less and less at American altars. "We face one another and join hands. Kneeling is being replaced by our more interactive, 'let's share' approach to spiritual matters..."[10] Years ago, Pentecostal Christians hardly even went to church without spending some time on their knees. It was common to kneel during prayer times, to come to an altar in response to the message and kneel. Dean Merrill, a global prayer leader confesses,
>
> When I get down on my knees to pray, the quality of my interaction with God is somehow changed...the biggest benefit is that kneeling reminds us who's who in the dialogue. Prayer is not a couple of fellows chatting about the Dallas Cowboys. It is a human being coming face to face with his or her Supreme Authority, the ineffable God who is approachable but still the One in charge.[11]

Crying out to God is the instinctive sense we have within us about the nature of God. He is a God of love, good and full of mercy.

Why would we pray to a God who did not love us? The absence of a clear conviction of God's love is an impediment to prayer. It is the enemy of faith, the antidote to hope. Love says, "He cares! And he is good!" And more specifically, "He cares about me, and if I pray, he will respond with grace and mercy."

> Always respond to every impulse to pray. The impulse to pray may come when you are reading or when you are battling with a text. I would make an absolute law of this—always obey such an impulse.
> — Martyn Lloyd-Jones

Faith in God's power is never enough. It is faith in his *character* that drives us to 'cry out' to Him. Robert Speer said,

> The evangelization of the world depends first of all upon a revival of prayer. Deeper than the need of men...aye, deep down at the bottom of our spiritless life is the need for the forgotten secret of prevailing, world-wide prayer.[12]

Intercession and the Heart of God

At Gethsemane, Jesus' intercessory cries rose to the Father. His *splagchnon* (the Greek word for 'compassion') spilled out onto the ground through tears of intercession. Intercession should overflow with deep inward affection, with God's tender mercies thundering up and out of our inward parts. When our *"bowels"* – a term the Bible uses for our innermost being – are filled with His *splagchnon*, the oppressed are set free. The language is suggestive of birth. God, by His sovereignty, places the need, the hurt, the pain, the promise of God with regard to some person or thing, some time or place, deep within us, as if we were "pregnant" with the possibility of what might change, who might be touched or saved, delivered or directed. And though, as with a pre-born child, that promise or potential is within us, it requires a live-birth! Intercession and travail, this mysterious collaboration with God in the Spirit, gives birth to such mysterious things. The will of God for the earth, for persons and nations, for places and things, travels through us – by the mystery of intercessory prayer.

Jesus Christ, as God, prayed, weeping for humanity. The Father responded in unity with the Son and *"arose to judgment, to deliver all the meek [oppressed] of the earth"* (Psalm 76:9). The groans of the children of Israel in the opening chapters of Exodus were received as prayers in heaven. *"God heard their groaning, God remembered...God looked...and God had respect [acknowledged them]"* (Exodus 2:24-25).

Epaphras prayed *"earnestly"* (Colossians 4:12). Andrew Bonar uses the phrase, "...with strong [fervent], great wrestling souls are won."[13] Paul asked the Romans to *"strive together"* in prayer. The word is *agonizomai* from which we get our word agony (Romans 15:30). It is the idea of "throwing the whole soul into praying."[14] In earnest prayer, we do not merely say a prayer. The whole of our being goes out in prayer. We are consumed by the prayer experience. Such prayer is often exhausting.

Praying is one thing but crying out to God with Holy desperation is another. It was when Israel *cried out* to God that He heard them. Throughout Scripture, from Israel's cries in slavery to blind Bartimaeus, crying out with holy desperation, puts us on the cusp of breakthrough.

> The devil is aware that one hour of close fellowship, hearty converse with God in prayer, is able to pull down what he hath been contriving and building many a year.
> — Flavel

E. M. Bounds says,

> To say prayers in a decent, delicate way is not heavy work. But to pray really, to pray till hell feels the ponderous stroke, to pray till the iron gates of difficulty are opened, till the

mountains of obstacles are removed, till the mists are exhaled and the clouds are lifted, and the sunshine of a cloudless day brightens – this is hard work, but it is God's work and man's best labor.[15]

When you were a child and found yourself injured or frightened, you cried out. Nothing is more motivating to a parent than the scream of a desperate child. Diminutive mothers are transformed into warriors in behalf of a distressed child.

Modern speech is full of forms, verbal phrases that are associated with everything from weddings to wills. Just a few words and we know the document and its intent "Dearly beloved, we are gathered together in the company of God and these witnesses to join…" – a *wedding*. And, "I, being of sound mind and judgment, do leave to…" – a *will*. Even if the words vary slightly, the *form* informs us about the *function*.

The Bible has forms as well, but because language changes, ancient forms and modern forms differ. Ancient prayers often had a distinctive 'form' to them as well. Though simple, scholars recognize the literary structure as an ancient plea form [form compliant and sensitive to cultural language norms]. The first *formal* prayer of the Bible is in Genesis 17:18, *"O, that Ishmael might live before me!"* The phrase is so simple that it doesn't seem possible that it is a formal plea. It is a prayer of Abraham, a tearful plea in the form of a prayer. It is the cry of a father in behalf of his estranged child.[16] Notice, form shouldn't deny passion – and it doesn't here. Prayer can be precise, but it should never be without heart. Great men of Christian history

> When I am praying the most eloquently, I am getting the least accomplished in my prayer life. But when I stop getting eloquent and give God less theology and shut up and just gaze upward and wait for God to speak to my heart He speaks with such power that I have to grab a pencil and a notebook and take notes on what God is saying to my heart.
>
> — A. W. Tozer

were men of passionate prayer.

- John Welsh spent eight of every twenty-four hours in prayer.
- David Brainerd rode through the American wilderness – praying as he went.
- "I retired early this morning into the woods for prayer; had the assistance of God's Spirit, and faith in exercise; and was enabled to plead with fervency for the advancement of Christ's kingdom in the world, and to intercede for dear, absent friends." David Brainerd
- John Wesley changed the face of England with bold and earnest prayer.[17]
- Jonathan Edwards recalled, "I rode out into the woods... as my manner had been to walk for divine contemplation and prayer, I had such a view that for me was extraordinary of the glory of the Son of God...this continued for an hour; and kept me the greater part of the time in a flood of tears and weeping aloud. I felt an ardency of soul to be what I know not otherwise how to express, emptied and annihilated; to love Him with a holy and pure love; to serve and follow Him; to be perfectly sanctified and made pure with a divine and heavenly purity."[18]

Prayer Precepts Taught by Jesus

- **ACCORDING TO THE DIVINE WILL OF GOD** – Every prayer should be submitted to the will of God. When we pray, according to His will, He hears us (1 John 5:14, 15). Praying according to His will is not simply an expression of our lips; it is the essence of a life lived in union with Him (John 15:7).
- **FAITH** – Without faith it is impossible to please God! (Mark 11:22-24; Hebrews 11:6; James 1:6,7) All things are possible to those who believe. Faith claims what it asks for.
- **FASTING** – Fasting is one of three disciplines in Matthew 6 to which Jesus ties a reward (Matthew 6:18). Fasting is the control point for all things internal. If you can say, "No!" to the most native desires of the flesh, food and sex, you have gained a great measure of control over the flesh. Jesus emphasized the triad of prayer, fasting and power (Matthew 9:15; 17:21; Mark 9:29). See also: Psalm 35:13; Nehemiah 1:4; Daniel 9:23; Luke 2:37; Acts 10:31; 13:3; 14:23; 1 Corinthians 7:5.
- **FORGIVENESS** – Four times in the Sermon on the Mount, Jesus emphasizes forgiveness. Unless we forgive, we will not be forgiven! If we understood the offense of sin and holiness of God, we might perceive more accurately the value of forgiveness. An unpayable debt, an unthinkable record of sin, an offense so great that it cost God His Son—that's our sin. That He would forgive is an introduction to the shocking grace of God. So sobering should that forgiveness be to us, that we are now ready to forgive such slight sins against us. Great as they are, the offenses of others to us can't compare to our offense against His holiness. (Matthew 5:22-26, 44-45; 6:14; 18:21, 35; Mark 11:35).
- **HUMILITY** – God resists the proud, but he gives grace to the humble (2 Chronicles 7:14; 34:27; Luke 18:9-14; James 4:6; Matthew 26:20-23).
- **IN THE DIVINE NAME** – The Old Testament Jew revered the unspeakable name of Yahweh. He would not even write it, so holy was the name of God. We also, as Christians, honor the name of Yahweh. And consistent with the Old Testament pattern, we revere the name of Jesus in the same way. We pray to God, the Father, who hears and answers prayer (Matthew 6:6, 9; John 15:16). We also pray to God, the Son, and we see Him as co-equal with the Father (Acts. 7:59; 9:13-17; Romans 10:12). Modernists who want to deny Christians the right to pray in the name of Jesus but allow other faiths to utter the names of their gods, don't understand – Jesus is God! To deny prayer to Jesus or to deny

prayer to the Father in His name is a demand that Christians deny Jesus Christ as God! That is unacceptable. There is no Biblical instance of prayer to the Holy Spirit. And yet there is ample evidence of fellowship with and in the Spirit. Communion with the Spirit naturally suggests an on-going conversation with the resident of our hearts—God, the Holy Ghost (Romans 8:26, 27). He enables us to pray. He quickens our hearts. He illuminates our praying. We are caught up on the Spirit (Revelation 1:10) and we pray and hear from heaven. We pray with the enabling of the Spirit, through and in the name of the Son, to the Father. Access to heaven is gained by whispering the "secret name" of Jesus (Matthew 7:22; 18:19, 20; John 14:13, 14; 15:7, 16; 16:23, 24, 26; Acts. 3:6; Ephesians 5:20). Prayer "in the Name" – a singular form indicates the unity of the God-head, Father, Son and Holy Spirit (Matthew 28:19). Prayer "in the name" is not simply a form of speech. It is rather a frame of mind (Matthew 10:26; 18:5; Acts. 3:16). We say "in the name of Jesus" as if to convert an unworthy request to a worthy one. Praying "in the name" is praying with a right motive, not a right phrase. It means that Jesus is Lord of the life uttering the name. It means that we intend for our request to further the purposes of His kingdom and not some narrow selfish ambition. It means that we believe we are praying as He would pray, according to all that He is in Himself.

- ♦ **IN THE SPIRIT** – Prayer in or enabled by the Spirit is God-assisted praying. It is dependence on Him. It is allowing the Holy Spirit to express the will of God for our lives, for some situation, for the earth itself, through us. It is a compensation for our weakness. It is an attempt to align our prayers with the will of God. It is a conscious attempt to allow ourselves to be utterly and completely influenced by the Spirit when we pray. (Ephesians 6:18; Jude 20; Romans 8:9, 26, 27). Andrew Murray says, "The Spirit breathing, the Son's intercession, the Father's will – there, three become one in us."[19]
- ♦ **OBEDIENCE** – He gives the Holy Spirit to those who obey Him. Obedience is the fruit that emerges from a life that truly acknowledges Jesus as Lord (Romans 6:16, 17; Deuteronomy 11:13; John 14:14, 15; 1 John 3:22)
- ♦ **PERSISTENCE** – Persistence is the Jacob mode of prayer. It is praying until you pray through. It is not letting go of God until He answers. It is importunity – which means "shamelessness!" I refuse to be ashamed of my passionate will-not-be-denied posture in prayer. It is the friend in the middle willing to disturb the friend with plenty, even if the time

is midnight. He will not be turned away empty. Despite resistance, he refuses to go away until he has an answer. (Luke 11:5-10; 18:1-8; Ephesians 6:18).

- **PRIVACY**[20] – Jesus talked about praying behind a shut door (Matthew 6:6). Perhaps it is the idea of locking yourself in to God. Public praying for show was condemned by Jesus (Matthew 6:5). Mechanical and pretentious prayers were also rejected (Mark 12:40). Jesus sought solitude when He prayed (Luke 6:12). Alone, you can pour out your heart to God. Alone, you have a private meeting in which uncensored thoughts and motives can be freely expressed and corrected. Alone, you lay aside inhibitions and become authentically transparent. Alone, you weep and cry out to God. Alone, you purify your soul and renew your sight.

- **REPENTANCE** – The prodigal found acceptance from the Father when he returned home with a repentant heart (Luke 15:18, 21). Sin creates a separation between us and God. Repentance is the essential step to remove the blockage of sin 2 Kings 8:33, 34; Jeremiah 36:7; Acts 8:22; Nehemiah 1:4-7; Daniel 9:4-11; Luke 18:13.

- **SINCERITY** – The Pharisees made a mockery of prayer (Matthew 6:5, 15). Sincerity is the absence of pretense. No hypocrisy. It is the badge of authenticity. I am what I am before God – nothing more and nothing less. John 4:24; Psalms 42:1.

1. P. Douglas Small, *Transforming Your Church into A House of Prayer* (Cleveland, TN: Pathway Press, 2006), 103.
2. George Barna, *The Index of Leading Spiritual Indicators*, 77.
3. Ibid, 106.
4. Susan Gaddis. *Intercessors: God's End-Time Vanguard* (Pathway Press: Cleveland, TN; 1999), 21.
5. Bill Thrasher, *Victorious Praying* (Moody: Chicago; 2003), 41.
6. E.M. Bounds, *The Best of E. M. Bounds*, 47.
7. Small, *Transforming Your Church into A House of Prayer*.
8. Ibid.
9. Martin Smith, "The Body at Prayer," *The Contemporaries Meet The Classics on Prayer*, ed. Leonard Allen (West Monroe, LA: Howard Publishing, 2003), 138-139.
10. Dean Merrill, "Whatever Happened to Kneeling?" *The Contemporaries Meet The Classics on Prayer*, ed. Leonard Allen (West Monroe, LA: Howard Publishing, 2003), 141.
11. Ibid, 142.
12. Quoted by Robert Speer in *Union Seminary Magazine* (Union Theological Seminary, 1896), 46.
13. Herbert Lockyer, *All the Prayers of the Bible* (Grand Rapids, MI: Zondervan, 1959), 253.
14. Ibid, 255.
15. Bob Griffin, *Firestorms of Revival* (Lake Mary, FL: Strang Publications, 2006), 140.
16. Lockyer, 22.
17. Lockyer, 268.
18. Bounds, *The Best of E. M. Bounds*, 55.
19. Adapted from Lockyer, Section: "Prayer in the Precepts of Christ," 175-180.
20. Eugene Peterson says, "Solitude in prayer is not privacy. The differences between privacy and solitude are profound. Privacy is our attempt to insulate the self from interference; solitude leaves the company of others for a time in order to listen to them more deeply, be aware of them, serve them. Privacy is getting away from others so that I don't have to be bothered with them; solitude is getting away from the crowd so that I can be instructed by the still, small voice of God, who is enthroned on the praises of the multitudes. Private prayers are selfish and thin; prayer in solitude enrolls in a mult-voiced, century-layered community; with angels and archangels in all the company of heaven we sing, 'Holy, Holy, Holy, Lord God Almighty.'" See: "Solitude, Not Privacy," *The Contemporaries Meet The Classics on Prayer*, ed. Leonard Allen (West Monroe, LA: Howard Publishing, 2003), 223.

SECTION FOUR
Back to the Future

CHAPTER 13
Nation Changing Prayer

OUR NATIONAL SPIRITUAL HISTORY

There have been four great spiritual awakenings in North American history. The First Great Awakening started in the 1730s. It reached its peak around 1740-1743 and still had some impetus as late as the 1760s. It provided the context for the American Revolution. It was the first galvanizing experience that diverse Americans had shared together. Suddenly, those who came here to champion a slice of Christianity dissimilar to another denomination's version of faith found themselves shoulder to shoulder, listening to Whitefield and Wesley.

In those moments, they came to realize that while there were differences between the various streams of Christianity – differences that had been persecuted in Europe, there was also a common center, and the atmosphere here was more conciliatory, more congenial – though not without some exceptions. Still, they begin to reckon that their odds of attaining true freedom would be found in a new tethering of their colonies, rather than to England. Defining moments and issues would be the motivator, but were it not for the faith bond, no Revolution would have come.

The Second Great Awakening came in the early 1800s with the camp-meetings of Kentucky. Finney's ministry is considered a part of that era as was the renewal that swept America's colleges. Significant numbers of blacks attended camp-meeting events. It is generally thought that this awakening gave impetus to the abolition movement. Lincoln had exposure to camp-meetings in the wilderness of Illinois. The camp-meetings spread throughout parts of Tennessee and into the Carolinas.

The Third Great Awakening occurred in 1857-1858. It was a marketplace awakening, and some say, it had the greatest impact of all. It spread across the continent in a wave of packed noon-time

> ### A Man of Prayer in A Pagan Government
> Daniel served pagan empires and he did so without compromise. His life was marked by uncompromising prayer. Notice these elements of Daniel's prayer life (Daniel 9):
>
> | | |
> |---|---|
> | He had a place of prayer | "he went into his house." |
> | He prayed with courage | "his windows being opened." |
> | He had a point of focus | "toward Jerusalem (the temple)" |
> | His attitude was humility | "he kneeled upon his knees." |
> | His habit was consistent | "he prayed three times a day." |
> | He had a grateful disposition | he "gave thanks before his God." |
> | He persisted | ... "as he did aforetime." |
>
> Daniel prayed to the God of Israel, "My God...Our God" (9:8, 17, 18). He recognized God as above time (6:26). He knew Him as a God of forgiveness (9:9, 18, 19) and fidelity (9:11, 13). God was true to his promises and he delivered those who called by His name (9:19). He recognized the presence of angels (9:21; Zech. 1; Luke 1:19-26) interacting with prayer.

prayer gatherings. Cities came to a stop for prayer. And in the days of the War Between the States, the revival ran through the Southern Army.

In 1906, came the great Azusa Street Revival. Feeding the Azusa Street Revival was the awakening in Wales, led by Evan Roberts. Joseph Smale, pastor of First Baptist Church in Los Angeles was following the Wales revival and urging prayer and awakening. His church resisted the movement, but a number of its members were participants in the Asuza Street outpouring. News of Azusa Street rapidly circled the earth. It was also an extension of the holiness revivals of the 1800s – a call to consecration and sanctification, a desire for an empowered life in Christ. The fourth Great Awakening, though evangelical historians resist the application of the title, gave birth to the Pentecostal Movement. Out of it, came a variety of new denominations and movements which articulated a pneumatology that had been lost to the Church – a post-conversion encounter with Christ by the Spirit that empowers one for greater witness. Suddenly, apostolic gifts that had been virtually forgotten reappeared. The last century became the greatest, in terms of harvest, the Church had seen since the first century.

The First Great Awakening

In the first Great Awakening, Jonathan Edwards became a fresh vessel of purity and prayer in the hand of God. He was a part of movement of united prayer and pastoral covenants. He is best remembered for his message, "Sinners in the Hands of an Angry God!" – a politically incorrect sermon in any setting where sin abounds. Puritanism had declined. Godlessness, crime and immorality were flooding the colonies. The situation was dire. In most cities, the decent feared leaving their homes at night. The streets were filled with muggers and thieves. Deism was flowering. In the culture "the worst vices prevailed...if any one condemned them, he was set down as a fool..."[1]

With church rolls shrinking a generation before, ministers in New England had adopted the "Halfway Covenant." It allowed people who made no profession of faith to have their children baptized. These youngsters grew up without godly disciplines and soon there were more of them than genuinely professing believers in the church. "Halfway" converts eventually took communion and entered the ministry.[2] The result was a passionless and misdirected church, powerless to change culture. The spiritual decline was also impacted by the so-called Enlightenment. Most believed that only "united, earnest prayer could bring a divine outpouring" that would save the colonies. Ministers themselves began to call out to God in prayer, seeking his face, in order to lead their people into revival.[3] That's when God sent the first Great Awakening (1726-1756) to America. Without it, this would no doubt be a very different nation.[4]

Our National Beginnings

On the morning of September 7, 1774, the Continental Congress of the United States had its first session. On this historic occasion, Congress was opened with prayer. But this was no mere prayer, no simple and short invocation irrelevant to the actual proceedings. It was a three-hour prayer and Bible study event.

Contemporary historians want to convince us that these men were practically all atheists and secularists. Are we to believe that such men had a three-hour prayer meeting? Quite a feat, wouldn't you say? The study was from Psalm 35 and 36. John Adams wrote, "God spoke to Congress...and it built our faith." He called the morning, an extraordinary beginning of America's Congress. One witness said, "Even the stern old Quakers had tears running down their cheeks."[5]

The most active members of the Constitutional Congress were not Jefferson or Franklin, the well-known founders the secularists champion, neither of which were true deists or anti-Christian. Quite the contrary, but by the use of selective quotes, they have been positioned as 'the leaders' and as godless – certainly cool, if not hostile, to faith. It is nonsense.

> No man can do a great and enduring work for God who is not a man of prayer, and no man can be a man of prayer who does not give much time to praying.
> – E. M. Bounds

Governor Morris, a name rarely heard today, was the final man to sign the Constitution, afforded to him as an act of honor by his peers. He spoke on the floor 173 times, more than anyone else. The handwriting of the document is his penmanship. Morris said, "Religion is the only solid basis of good morals. Therefore, education should teach the precepts of religion and the duties of man toward God."[6] He is hardly the poster boy the liberals want, so they have rewritten history.

The second most active member of the Constitutional Congress was James Wilson. He declared, "Human law must rest its authority ultimately upon the authorship of that law which is divine…religion and law are twin sisters, they are friends, they are mutual assistants."[7]

Alexander Hamilton, another signer viewed with horror what was happening in France. What he recoiled at is now happening in this nation, and he would no doubt be aghast. Hamilton noted,

> The attempt, by the rulers of a nation (France) to destroy all religious opinion and to pervert a whole people to atheism is a phenomenon of profligacy (act of moral depravity) … To establish atheism on the ruins of Christianity is to deprive mankind of its best consolations and most animating hopes and to make a gloomy desert of the universe."[8]

Wonder what the founders would say today?

After the Revolutionary War, the nation again fell into moral decay. The ties with France brought a wave of anti-Christian influence. Voltaire boldly asserted, "Christianity will be forgotten in thirty years time." Shockingly, Supreme Court Justice John Marshall suggested that "the church is too far gone ever to be redeemed." Christians on college campuses convened in secret to avoid persecution. There was an epidemic of alcoholism. Then in 1794, churches of nearly all denominations rallied to a call for united agreement in prayer. The result was a ground swell that seeded the Second Great Awakening.[9]

The Second Great Awakening

During the second Great Awakening (1776-1810), the camp-meeting was a prominent vehicle for renewal. Rationalism had taken over colleges and universities. Godly professors were marginalized. Sceptics of the faith were enthroned as the enlightened. Christian students suffered as a growing minority. Higher education, institutions which had been founded as Bible Colleges, to train clergy, turned away from their Biblical roots. Infidelity was rampant and a ruin to families. The culture was characterized by "promiscuity, profanity, gambling, and drunkenness."[10] Doctrinal division and spiritual dullness plagued the churches. Prominent preachers were joined by lay leaders with white-hot hearts, as critical cultural change agents.[11]

Isaac Backus promoted the idea, "There is only one power on earth that commands the power of heaven – prayer."[12] He wrote "Pleas for Prayer for Revival of Religion." The pamphlet was distributed to churches of all denominations. The first Monday of every month became a day of prayer for national revival. The nation was mobilized to pray. In Kentucky, a four-day observance of the Lord's Supper provoked a revival. Three months later for a similar observance, twenty thousand showed up. Thousands were converted.[13] Youth were impacted. A new generation was claimed for God. Revival shook Yale College in 1802. The whole mass of students seemed destined to press into the Kingdom of God. Nearly all the converts from the revival entered the ministry.[14] "It was God's hour. Revival stopped scepticism in its tracks and returned the helm of the country to the godly."[15] Even the wild frontier full of gambling and vice was transformed. The lamb of Christianity, tamed the roaring lion of sin. The revival turned "drunkards, horse thieves, gamblers, cock fighters, and murderers into evangelists."[16]

Logan County, Kentucky had become a harbor for fugitives from the law. It was nicknamed Rogues' Harbor. Even there, after a Presbyterian minister named James McGready called three small congregations to solemn prayer and communion, crowds ranging from 10,000 to 25,000 gathered for revivals. These crowds gathered for days, listening to preaching and preparing their hearts to receive the elements of communion. By January of 1801, these great camp meeting revivals were spreading from county to county in Kentucky and Tennessee. Eyewitnesses wrote, "The roads were crowded with wagons, carriages, horses and footmen moving to

Prayers for Cities and Nations

- Genesis 18:23-33 – Abraham's prayer that God would save Sodom. The city was totally destroyed, but God remembered Abraham and spared the life of his nephew Lot (Genesis 19:29).
- Jonah 3 – Prayer in the city of Nineveh united in fasting, repentance and prayer and God did not destroy them.
- Daniel 9:1-19 – Daniel's prayer for the return of the Jews to their land.
- 2 Kings 19:15-19 – Hezekiah's prayer to save Jerusalem from the army of Assyria.
- 2 Chronicles 14:11 – Asa's prayer to save Jerusalem from a huge army of Ethiopians.

the solemn camp." Several preachers would be preaching at different places in the camp at the same time. Hundreds of people would be "struck down" at the same time. They would remain still for fifteen minutes. Some for as long as six-to-eight hours. At times the roar of people praying and crying out to God was like the sound of Niagara. People fell under the influence of deep conviction "as if a battery of a thousand guns had been opened upon them."[17] Helpless, before God's presence, they wept. They repented. And their lives were forever changed.

New York congregations joined in prayer. An awakening swept through Long Island in 1799. Infidelity was swept away. Taverns were deserted. Family feuds gave way to brotherly love. Some denominations quadrupled during this period. The American Bible Society and the American Tract Society were born. A number of Christian magazines began publication. The American Sunday School Union was created. The YMCA was launched. Historians say the Awakening again saved the nation from French rationalism, greed and godlessness, and from frontier violence.[18]

The Third Great Awakening

The third Great Awakening is called the Layman's Prayer Revival. It began in New York (1857-1858) as a noon-time prayer meeting, America needed a renewal. Crime was widespread. Banks were folding. The times were difficult, and the church was again ineffective.[19] The nation was in the middle of a gold rush. As gains grew in some sectors, godliness declined.

Jeremiah Lamphier felt the need for prayer and promoted idea of businessman's prayer meeting. Signs invited people to stop in for a few minutes. By 12:30, no one had showed up. Then Lamphier heard footsteps. First one and then another, until six had gathered for prayer. Twenty men came the next week, then forty.

The weekly meeting became daily. And that week, October 14, the nation had the greatest financial panic in history. Banks closed. Unemployment skyrocketed. Families were without food. Attendance at the prayer gathering swelled to more than 3000. Every sector of society showed up and sat together, praying.[20] Soon other prayer gatherings spread across the city, then across the nation. In six months, at least 10,000 businessmen were gathering in New York alone. Churches were full. Almost every public venue was crowded with people praying.

The Spirit of God settled on New York City. Sinners came to the prayer meetings. Thousands became devoted follows of Christ. Crime and vice drastically declined. The wealthy generously helped the poor. Ships coming into New York harbor came under the power of God's presence. On one ship, a captain and thirty men were converted to Christ before the ship docked. As sailors on one ship knelt for prayer, others mocked, but the power of God gripped them and they humbly knelt in repentance.

By March of 1858, from Maine to California, there was hardly a village or town to be found where 'a special divine power' did not appear displayed. In Chicago 2,000 men met at noon for prayer. In Philadelphia, 4,000 were meeting. "I have never, I think, been present at a more stirring and edifying prayer meeting…a divine influence seemed manifest…hearts melted…" one person reported."

In Waco, Texas, "Day and night the church has been crowded…Never before have we seen a whole community so effectually under a religious influence…thoroughly regenerated." Newspaper accounts of New Haven, Connecticut read, "City's Biggest Church Packed Twice Daily for Prayer" and "Revival Sweeps Yale." In Bethel, Connecticut, "Business Shuts Down for an Hour Each Day – Everybody Prays." In Albany, the headlines reported, "State Legislators Get Down on Knees." In Washington, D. C. the bold print read, "Five Prayer Meetings Go Round the Clock."[21] In cities all across the nation, signs went up at noon – "Closed for Prayer!" The whole nation seemed to be stopping for prayer. And God touched the nation.

> Prayer does not fit us for the greater work, prayer is the greater work.
> – Oswald Chambers

In Louisville, Kentucky, it was said, "The Spirit of God seems to be brooding over our city…" Every morning, a call to prayer in the legislature of New York drew crowds. Leading businessmen of Boston attended prayer meetings. One writer said, "'Publicans and sinners' are awakened, and are entering the prayer meetings of their own accord. Some of them manifest signs of sincere repentance." It was estimated that 50,000 people a week were being converted. Church membership leaped. The numbers indicate that one of every thirty citizens in the whole nation was swept into the church by the revival.[22] Honor was restored. Any business that injured the community was regarded as wrong. People began to be more honest, truthful and conscientious.

Azusa Street

In 1906, revival came to the humble livery stable at 312 Azusa Street in Los Angeles. On the morning of the San Francisco earthquake, Los Angeles was also rolled out of bed. Folks grabbed for a morning paper, but instead of news about the earthquake, the front page offered news about a different stirring – "Strange Babel of Tongues at Azusa Street." It seemed that the whole city wanted to investigate.

The meetings were held three times daily and at times twenty-four hours a day. They cut across socio-economic and racial barriers. It was Joel's prophecy fulfilled again, a Pentecostal infusion of power into an anaemic church. And yet, like the great revivals before it - repentance, humility, unity, prayer, waiting on God, and a hunger for holiness at its heart.

It quickly spread across the nation and around the world. Atlanta newspapers reported an amazing revival of prayer sweeping the city. The Supreme Court of Georgia, stores, factories, offices and even saloons closed their doors so people could attend noon prayer meetings. In one small Kentucky town, a thousand people came to Christ in less than two months. In Atlantic City, only fifty unconverted adults remained out of a population of 50,000. For two hours at midday, Denver was under a spell. The markets were deserted. The entire city was bowing before the throne of heaven. Whole cities were being impacted.

On college campuses, God was stirring youth. Bible study groups doubled at Cornell. Two thirds of the men at Northwestern University in Illinois enrolled in Bible classes. Two hundred men were converted at Trinity College, now Duke University, in North Carolina. Only a couple dozen of the whole student body was left unsaved.

God's people were praying. The Michigan Christian Advocate said, "A great revival is sweeping the United States. The Holy Spirit is convincing the people of sin, of righteousness and of judgment to come." Where prayer services were regularly held, they were charged with spiritual power. *The Baptist Home Mission Monthly* noted, "a quickening of spiritual impulse and life in the churches and in our own educational institution ... a remarkable responsiveness to the presentation of the claims of Christ upon the hearts and consciences of men."

Camp Creek

For two years, Pastor Richard Spurling prayed for revival. Nothing happened, but still he persisted. He longed for a revival that transcended differences between Christians, one that championed unity for the noble cause of renewal. Grateful for the Reformation, he nevertheless felt Luther had made a mistake by anchoring it more to truth than to love. It wasn't a frail code of behavior this proponent of holiness sought, indeed, he felt that the church was deeply compromised. Rather, it was truth dipped in love. It was the hard edge of principle paired with a loving spirit of reconciliation. A change was needed.

> Pentecost didn't come through a preaching service; Pentecost came to a prayer service. From Pentecost to Patmos, God never departs from the pattern.
> – Armin Gesswein

He broke with his Baptist flock and founded the Christian Union eight members strong. His vision, rising out of the remote corner of Tennessee near the North Carolina and Georgia boundaries, was breathtaking. He envisioned a global movement of holiness folk, filled with love not fight. The movement would emphasize intrinsic doctrines and assert the importance of Christian service. But the ultimate objective was "to restore primitive Christianity and bring about the union of all denominations."[23] Astonishing, given the rural mountain context form wich such a vision emerged.

Spurling longed for deeper blessings from God and the supernatural enablement he saw in the Biblical text. After ten more years of prayer, in 1986, revival came. And out of that revival, the denomination in which I serve, the Church of God, was formed. With almost 40,000 churches, missions and preaching stations in 183 nations, Spurling could have never guessed how God would answer his prayers.

The late Charles Conn, historian, writes of the revival that launched the movement,

> In distant counties the plowing was stopped at midday; the churning was left sour in the crocks; the cows were milked while the sun was high; and the oxen were given hasty provender, and the wagons headed over the hills toward Camp

Creek...Great throngs crowded around the schoolhouse, teeming out into the near-by woods, the holiness people 'prayed, and shouted, and exhorted until hundreds of hard sinners were converted.' Besides the hundreds that were converted and filled with the Holy Ghost, many afflicted people were healed. The diseases and sicknesses that were cured...are said to be miraculous.[24]

The social moral influence was significant as well.

Lives that had been disorderly became upright; men who had been violent became meek; drunkards quit their drinking... Holiness to them was not a utopian ideal, but a practical way of living made possible by a divine work of sanctification."[25]

In small towns, one after another, preachers full of the spirit went forth telling the story. Awakenings became normal happenings declaring, "Jesus is alive!" with demonstrations of his life-giving power. Persecution could not slow the explosive growth. Common men with limited education preached from well-worn marked up Bibles. Calloused knees and unflinchingly bold faith stood cities down. Resisters became members. The rowdy were humbled. The climate of whole cities was affected.

Needed! Another Great Awakening

In the last hundred years, we have had significant national spiritual moments, short of a Great Awakening. In the 1940's and '50's we experienced the signs and wonders revival. In that same era, Billy Graham became a national phenomenon. The Pentecostal World Conference was also born at the turn of the half century. Shortly after that, staid denominations began to feel the impact of Pentecost. By the 1960s and '70s, every Christian denomination had been visited by the Charismatic renewal. During the same era, "the Jesus movement" captured the hearts of dissident youth and exploded onto the national scene. It has been almost thirty years since the fires of that renewal began to fade.

Revival is the work of God in the Church among His people. Awakening is the work of God in a culture that has forgotten Him, His Word or His Love. The typical revival has a three-to-five year life-cycle, and is often confined to the church, according to some renewal experts. A Great Awakening is a macro-revival, culture-wide and nation impacting. It begins in the church, sometimes with one man and woman, and breaks out into the community, impacting the region, at times a nation. Awakenings adjust the national moral and spiritual bearings, not for a few years, but for a generation. Their indirect impact is twice as long. Our nation is in trouble again. Nothing short of a Great Awakening can save the nation now.

In 1787, Alexander Tyler, a Scottish historian wrote,

> A democracy is always temporary in nature; it simply cannot exist as a permanent form of government...the average age of the world's greatest civilizations – from the beginning of history – has been about 200 years. During those 200 years, these nations always progressed...From bondage to spiritual faith; from spiritual faith to great courage; from courage to liberty; from liberty to abundance; from abundance to complacency; from complacency to apathy; from apathy to dependence; and from dependence back to bondage.[26]

1. Henry Johnson, *Stories of Great Revivals* (London: The Religious Tract Society, 1906), 21-22.
2. *America's Great Revivals*, (Minneapolis, MN; Bethany House – A division of Baker), 6, 9.
3. Malcolm McDow and Alvin L. Reid, *Fire Fall: How God Has Shaped History Through Revivals* (Nashville: Broadman and Holman Publishers, 1997), 205.
4. Bob Griffin, *Firestorms of Revival* (Lake Mary, FL: Strang Publications, 2006), 110.
5. David Barton, "America's Founding Fathers: Were they Christian?" Bill Perkins, ed. *Steeling the Mind of America* (New Leaf Press: Green Forest, AR; 1997), 27.
6. Ibid, 16.
7. Ibid, 17.
8. *Gleanings of David Barton* <www.christianparents.com/preserve.htm>.
9. Dale A. Robbins, "Don't Give Up On America!" (Victorious Publications: Grass Valley, CA; 1995). See also: <www.victorious.org/prayamer.htm>.
10. McDow and Reid, 228.
11. Griffin, 111.
12. Mary Stewart Relfe, *Cure of All Ills* (Montgomery, AL: League of Prayer, 1988), 27.
13. Winke Pratney, *Revival* (Springfield, PA: Whitaker House, 1983), 112-114.
14. Warren A. Chandler, *Great Revivals and the Great Republic* (Nashville, TN: Publishing House of the M. E. Church, 1904), 189.
15. Pratney, 115, 134-135.
16. Relfe, 35.
17. *America's Great Revivals*, 41.
18. Griffin, 205; See also McDow and Reid, 247.
19. Griffin, 112.
20. *America's Great Revivals*, 55.
21. Ibid, 64.
22. Ibid, 68-69.
23. Charles Conn. *Like a Mighty Army* (Pathway: Cleveland, TN; 1955), 7.
24. Ibid, 26-27.
26. Griffin, 29.

CHAPTER 14
Looking for a Vessel

SUCH A PLEASANT PLACE

It was Elijah's last day on the earth (2 Kings 2). Elisha had refused to leave him. They had journeyed from Gilgal to Bethel and back to Jericho. They had crossed the Jordan after it had been miraculously parted with Elijah's mantle. The sons of the prophets were in tow. And then, a chariot of fire swept down to the earth from another world, and Elijah was gone. Left behind was the symbol of his prophetic anointing – his mantle. Elisha clutched it as his own. He smote the Jordan and it parted again. The sons of the prophets gasped, *"The spirit of Elijah is on Elisha"* (v. 15).

Returning toward Jericho, the men of the city seized the moment. They needed a miracle for their town. They explained their dilemma. *"This is such a pleasant place. But the water is bitter and there is no fruit"* (v. 19).

Bad Water

If you have ever sipped fruit juice in balmy Jericho, you have to agree, it is "such a pleasant place." Yet, the water was not merely bad. The water was deadly. Their children were dying due to the poison water. The toxic water was also destroying their harvest. There was no fruit.

Why would you call any place, despite its climate and charm, pleasant, if your children were dying and there was no harvest? We have just described America! It is "such a pleasant place." Our kids are dying. The spiritual water here is killing them. We have not had a harvest in forty years. The rate of church closures is alarming. Across the spectrum, America's churches are not keeping pace with population growth of 12.2 percent. The net increase is marginal. Approximately 3,000 churches closed every year in the last decade. While new churches were started, the net increase in this century is only 800 each year. When population growth is used as the benchmark, the deficit is almost 10,000 new churches now needed. The U.S. Census predicts a population of 520 million in 2050. At the current growth trajectories, the church will increasingly lose ground, inferring that we are a nation that in past generations knew God. Seventy-percent of Christians are in spiritual survival mode, according to church analyst, Lyle Schaller. Only three to five percent are in a "kingdom building mode."[1]

A *U.S. News and World Report* cover story carried the headline noting, "Cheating, Writing and Arithmetic: A New Epidemic

> **Prayer Walking**
>
> God promised Abraham the land under which the soles of his feet trod. He obediently walked, and God awarded him real estate. Though he never acquired the deed to the land, can there be any doubt that his name is all over the sliver of ground we call the Holy Land? Prayer-walking is not magic. But it is a means of pushing prayer into the streets. It wakes up hearts. If we are living temples and if our hearts are altars, could it be that prayer walking is a means of leaving the incense of his fragrance all over the city. Choose your geographic area. Send prayer walkers in teams of two or three, but no more. Have them pray as they walk, with their eyes open. They pray conversationally, one at a time. They may need to record their impressions. They are in the neighborhood to bless.

of Fraud is Sweeping Though Our Schools."[2] Eight-thousand kids are contracting a sexually transmitted disease (STD) every day in America. One such STD is responsible for 99 percent of all cervical cancers in the nation. We have sown to the wind and we are now in the midst of a deadly killer storm.[3]

Pornography in America brings in $51 billion annually.[4] The church itself has been plagued by moral scandals. Less than half of the American population has "a lot of confidence" in the church.[5] We have lost social influence. Our moral reputation is tarnished.

Those who do attend church are increasingly disappointed with their worship experience – a whopping combined 48 percent. The assessments include terms like – "outdated," "just a performance," "boring," "disappointing," "embarrassing."[6] George Barna says, "Increasingly, faith commitment is viewed as a hobby rather than as a necessity for personal wholeness."[7] The late Bill Bright lamented about the church,

> It is asleep. Polluted with the desires and materialism of the world, she knows little about spiritual discipline and living the Spirit-filled life. She is complacent and at ease, thinking she has everything and is in need of nothing...a mirror image of the churches of Ephesus and Laodicea."[8]

Only eight percent of Americans are atheist, but they are more passionate in fighting something and someone they say doesn't exist than the church is in standing forthright for the resurrected Christ.

Nancy Leigh DeMoss describes the current church in bleak terms.

> The floodgates of unholiness – including willful, presumptuous, blatant sin – have opened up within the church. Adultery, drunkenness, abuse, profanity, outbursts of temper, divorce, pornography, immodest dress – such sins among professing believers – often members in good standing of respected local churches – are no longer rare exceptions.
>
> And then there are the more "respectable" forms of sewage that are often overlooked and tolerated among believers – things like overspending, unpaid debts, gluttony, gossip,

greed, covetousness, bitterness, pride, critical spirits, backbiting, temporal values, self-centeredness, and broken relationships. Sadly, the church – the place that is intended to showcase the glory and holiness of God – has become a safe place to sin.[9]

Witchcraft and cultic arts are flooding into the society. The Harry Potter series has become a primer in public schools for induction into the dark spirit-world. It is viewed as a fictional fantasy for Americans, a harmless intellectual escape. From such journeys into darkness, some do not return the same way. Though 58 percent of Americans reject the existence of Satan, he is nevertheless real. He does lurk in the darkness.

Israel was plagued by its temptation to flirt with dark spiritual powers. And it was always a costly departure from true faith. America is now being seduced. The preferred faith for our teens is now witchcraft. The church is keeping only four percent of its teens. One in five Americans are now aligned with New Age belief systems, some simultaneously active church members. The church itself is being shaped by New Age viewpoints. The journey within is replacing the yearning for the God, Most High. Questions about the meaning of life and the universe itself, about the power of self and the potential for the paranormal are preoccupying young adults. "The result is that psychology has become the vehicle for an emerging form of religiousness…"[10] The pyschologizing of faith in order to legitimize it and re-present it to society in a more palatable way assumes that in its original state it is unpresentable. This is tragic tactical error on the part of the contemporary church. It is not "the faith" that needs to be re-formed. It is the church.

Breaking the Spell

William Bridges in his classic book, *Managing Transitions*, says the difference between *disillusionment* and *disenchantment* is the key to change. Disillusionment, he says, causes us to recoil at defeat or failure, regroup and then try the same thing again. It causes pastors to move from one church to another only to repeat the same pattern. Parishioners hope a new pastor will lead them to the revival they have longed for. Both are disappointed.

Disillusionment will never fix the problem. Working with the same toolkit and the same mindset, we are "enchanted" with the notion that we left out one component in the last strategic plan. So we do essentially the same thing over and over again! With the same failed principles, we are destined to a similar dismal outcome.

Disenchantment is different. It steps outside the systemic model in which we have thought and lived. It refuses to work with the same tired presuppositions. It throws off "the spell." Spiritual warfare is an insidious thing. If it were tagged with Satan's initials clearly posted, it would easier to combat. Among his most effective strategies are thinking patterns (1 Cor. 10:4-5) that are so commonly accepted that we fail to see the evil with which they are laced. In denial, and unwilling to consider the possibility that his schemes and devices have imperceptibly infiltrated and influenced our own thinking, discernment fails.

What we have been doing for the last forty years has not been working. We are loosing the whole culture. And it is happening "on our watch!" Einstein once said, "You cannot solve the problem with the same level of intelligence that created it." We have step outside of our systems and consider new wineskins.

THE REALITY OF OUR SITUATION
Cultural Hostility Toward Faith

We are beyond complacency and apathy. Something has gone wrong. We are at war with the faith of our founding fathers. We are at war with decent Christians and their values.

- Rabbi Leslie Gutterman was chosen to pray at the Providence, Rhode Island public school graduation. The officials wanted a politically correct prayer. The Rabbi made a mistake. He said, "God!" three times. There was a lawsuit. The case went all the way to the Supreme Court. In a 5-4 verdict, they concluded that the prayer was coercive. A student, they said, hearing the word "God" might feel psychological pressure to conform to some religious or moral principle.[11] Incredible!

- Pastor Richard Parker was ready to pray the invocation at the Warren County, Virginia Board of Supervisors. Just before he prayed, the county attorney whispered to him not to say "Jesus." The terms "Lord" or "God" were permissible, but not "Jesus." The pastor refused to pray under such a restraint. Late-hour ambushes are frequently the tactics of the liberal left.

- A school teacher was ordered that his personal Bible could not be seen by students, and also ordered 237 books removed from the classroom library which referenced Christianity.[12]

- A Houston teacher tossed the Bibles of two students in the trash and marched them to the Principal's office. He threatened to involve Child Protective Services in an attempt to prove some type of parental incompetence manifest by the student's possession and obvious love of the Bible. The faith of the kids was offensive, an obstacle to his own classroom agenda.

- A ninth-grader received the grade of zero on a research project. Her topic was inappropriate. She wrote on – "Jesus!" Her teacher refused to allow a substitute project.

- In Stein v. Oshinsky (1962, and Collins v. Chandler Unified School District (1981), freedom of speech and the press was upheld for students unless their topic was religious. On that subject, constitutional free speech, the court ruled is not guaranteed. It is unconstitutional.[13]

- In St. Louis, a student was caught and charged for "praying" over his lunch. Physically lifted from his seat and reprimanded in front of all, he was told to never pray at the school again.
- In Ohio v. Whisner (1976), the Board of Education was refused the right to use or refer to the word "God" in any official writing.[14]
- In New Jersey, an honor guard was fired for saying, "God bless you and this family" at a graveside service in a Veteran's Cemetery.
- A state-employee in Minnesota was denied a access to the parking lot because of two bumper stickers on his car. One said, "God is a loving and caring God." Another, "God defines marriage as a union between a man and a woman."
- In McKinney, Texas, a pastor was charged with violating zoning laws. He had couples in his home for prayer and Bible study. The same city allowed home gatherings for watching football, having a party, or selling Tupperware – but not to gather to pray![15]

Most of these extraordinary and outrageous attacks of faith were noted by the late Chuck Colson on his Breakpoint radio program. The Liberty Legal Institute of Texas has documented hundreds of similar religious freedom violations in our nation. On October 20, 2004, it presented the Senate Judiciary Sub-committee a fifty-one page report entitled, "Examples of Religious Hostility in the Public Square."

Laws proliferate in a lawless society. In fifty state legislatures and our federal Congress, we have introduced 170,000 new civil laws.[16] That is aside from local ordinances and legal codes enacted by county commissioners and city-councils. We are drawing lines everywhere to stop foul play. All such efforts will fall flat. They are futile attempts to replace the moral lines of right and wrong that should be drawn on the inner walls of our hearts. Laws will never restrain a godless people. Outside pressure will never the take the place of internal restraint.

Moralist Alan Keyes reminds us, "What started out as separation of church and state has now been elevated into the separation of public life from morality."[18] It is a prescription for the complete breakdown of the culture. Arnold Toynbee, the great historian said, "History teaches us that when a barbarian race confronts a sleeping culture, the barbarian always wins."[19]

> Nothing would turn the nation back to God so surely and so quickly as a Church that prayed and prevailed. The world will never believe in a religion in which there is no supernatural power. A rationalized faith, a socialized Church, and a moralized gospel may gain applause, but they awaken no conviction and win no converts.[17]
> – Samuel Chadwick

Dirty Vessels Without Salt

George Barna compared the lifestyles of Christians and non-Christians using 131 different measures of attitudes, behaviors, values and beliefs. He found no visible differences between people of faith and non-believers.[20]

The church was to be as powerful a catalyst as is salt and as penetrating and visible as light in the darkness.[21] It is currently neither salt nor light. So, we are having virtually no measurable community impact. William Penn declared at the time of our nation's founding, "Let men be good, and the government cannot be bad… but if men be bad, the government will never be good."[22] Penn and the other founders knew, wicked men don't obey righteous laws.

Where is the clean vessel and the salt to purify the well? Elijah needed both a fresh vessel and salt!

ECHOES FROM THE PAST AND DISTANT SOUNDS
Cycles of Revival

When the prophets predicted the fall of Israel, no one believed them. How could the nation perish? But it happened. The American experiment has lasted for 250 years. In the same period, France has gone through seven constitutions. Like Israel, we believe, "This nation could never fall!" Could it? Could this nation cease to be tolerant of the very faith that its founders came here to practice – Christianity? Could persecution come here?

Winston Churchill declared that England needed "a supreme recovery of moral health and martial vigor." America is now in the same position. Like a ship taking on water, it is listing. It is guilty of the sins of other nations. It has lost the power of salt and light. Dr. Erwin W. Lutzer, Pastor of Moody Church admonishes, "We cannot be inundated by worldly values and yet meet our responsibility of keeping society from decay. How can we do it if we ourselves are guilty of the same sins? We must be brought to our knees and only then can God give us spiritual victories. The greatest need for the church today is believing prayer."

The day before he died, Dr. J. Edwin Orr, a Christian historian of great revivals on culture, preached a message entitled, "Revival Is Like Judgment Day."[23] What we call revival involves manifestations that intrigue us, sensations that thrill us and sermons that inspire us. True revival is likely to plow up our fields and uproot our lives, to disorder traces of sin and evidence of selfishness. True revival is likely to cause uncomfortable disclosures and call for unpleasant changes that create awkward transitions in lives that we have arranged largely for our own comfort. True revival will cost us. True revival will kill us – and that is the only way that revival will translate into lasting cultural impact.

Spurgeon said, "Make much of the cross."[24] Genuine revival is "always a revival of holiness" in which "people weep uncontrollably, and worse." It involves "a terrible conviction of sin." There is no authentic revival without "tears of conviction and sorrow."[25] In Brian Edward's classic book, he says:

> You cannot read far into the story of a revival without discovering that not only is prayer part of the inevitable result of an outpouring of the Spirit, but from a human standpoint, it is also the single most significant cause.[26]

Matthew Henry, the Commentator noted, "When God intends great mercy for His people, the first thing he does is set them a-praying."[27] Pastor Yonggi Cho has written a book, *Prayer, the Key to Revival*. He should know. His praying church numbers close to 800,000 members. The average church member in America spends more time in a single day watching television than is spent in an entire week pursuing spiritual matters.[28] Watchman Nee believed,

> If anyone should continue on in performing the work of prayer, he will become a channel for the will of God. Whenever the Lord has anything to do, He will seek that person out. Let me say this, that the will of God is always in search of a way out. The Lord is always apprehending someone or some people to be the expression of His will. If many will rise up to do this work, He will do many things because of their prayers.

R. A. Torrey offers a thundering reminder, "There have been revivals without much preaching, but there has never been a mighty revival without mighty prayer."[29] S. D. Gordon says, "You can do more than pray after you have prayed, but you cannot do more than pray until you have prayed…Prayer is striking the winning blow…service is gathering up the results."[30]

Sounds of Awakening

Could a Great Awakening happen again? Could whole cities be changing? It appears to be happening under our noses without our notice.

Looking for a Vessel

Almolonga

Almolonga, a small town in the Mayan highlands of Guatemala, George Otis writes, was:

> ...idolatrous, inebriated and economically depressed. Burdened by fear and poverty, the people sought support in alcohol and a local idol name Maximon. Determined to fight back, a group of local intercessors got busy, crying out to God during evening prayer vigils.[31]

The consequence of intense and persistent prayer was incredible. Ninety-percent of the town's citizens came to Christ. They repudiated their idolatrous connections. They local economy flourished. The town had suffered from poverty and violence. Each morning, drunken men were found lying in the streets still incapacitated from the night before. It was a city full of domestic violence with constant unrest and the four jails always over-crowed. That town has changed.

Churches and Christians had been persecuted. Evangelists were sometimes run out of town. But after a series of five-hour prayer vigils which involved spiritual declarations of freedom over the city, deliverance came to those under Satanic power. Healings revealed God's life-giving power. Now churches fill the city, often in places where bars were once housed. The jails are now closed, no longer needed. The fields around the city have become amazingly fertile and are nicknamed, "America's Vegetable Garden." Five-pound beets and carrots larger than a man's arm have been grown. Cabbages as large as basketballs are a part of the one-thousand percent increase in agricultural productivity.

The whole city gathered for prayer – 15,000 believers. They packed their main street and hung from balconies. A city in prayer. A city changed – transformed![32] Could that happen in America?

Cali, Columbia

Cali, Columbia was home to the infamous drug cartel. Seven-hundred to one-thousand tons of cocaine a year rolled out of the city to America and Europe. The cartel represented the most, well-organized criminal effort in global history. Blood flowed daily with a dozen or more murders. Looking at someone the wrong way could get one killed. Car bombs were common. Assassinations were ordered by the cartel and carried out with deadly diligence.

Every institution in the city was under the direct or indirect control of the cartel – banks, businesses, politicians on their pay-roll, police. Pastors were divided. Attempts at united prayer had failed. In the midst of this chaos, Julio Ruibal and his wife Ruth called their congregation to "prayer, unity and holiness." Their efforts sparked the idea of a joint prayer event for the city. They overly optimistically hoped for a few thousand. But the desperate city sensed the need for prayer. And 25,000 people came. The mayor was present, "Cali belongs to Jesus Christ," he declared. The crowd stayed until 6:00 a.m. Forty-eight hours later, the daily newspaper reported, "No Homicides!" It was a first.

In the next few months, the cartel came unhinged. Almost 1,000 cartel-soft police officers were exposed and fired. Intercessors begin to dream about cartel members themselves being arrested. Six weeks later the government launched a campaign against top cartel leaders. Helicopters buzzed the city. Police roadblocks were everywhere. In a short time, all seven cartel leaders were apprehended.

Such victories are rarely without a price. This battle was not merely moral and political. The cartel had been summoning the Pythoness of Cali, a well-known and powerful medium. The group was in spiritual-warfare. The Cartel became aware of the prayer efforts. A hit man took down Pastor Rubial as he arrived for a pastor's

> **HOW TO PRAY FOR YOUR GOVERNMENT OFFICIALS**
>
> Dr. Charles Stanley, pastor of First Baptist Church in Atlanta, Georgia, has suggested ten ways to pray for those who occupy the highest offices in the land.
>
> 1. Pray that they would realize their personal sinfulness and their need for Jesus Christ.
> 2. Pray that they would recognize their own inadequacy to fulfill their tasks and that they would depend upon God for knowledge, wisdom, and the courage to do what is right.
> 3. Pray that they would reject all counsel that violates spiritual principles, trusting God to prove them right.
> 4. Pray that they would resist those who would pressure them to violate their conscience.
> 5. Pray that they would reverse the trends of socialism and humanism in this nation, both of which deify man rather than God.
> 6. Pray that they would be ready to sacrifice their personal ambitions and political careers for the sake of this nation, if yielding them would be in the best interest of their country.
> 7. Pray that they would rely upon prayer and the Word of God as the source of their daily strength, wisdom and courage.
> 8. Pray they would restore dignity, honor, trustworthiness, and righteousness to the office they hold.
> 9. Pray that they would remember to be good examples in their conduct to the fathers, mothers, sons, and daughters of this nation.
> 10. Pray that they would be reminded daily that they are accountable to Almighty God for the decisions they make.

meeting. Ruth, his wife recalls the crimson color of her husband's blood spilled on the sidewalk – a modern martyr. Julio's death forged a unity among the pastors that was needed. Two-hundred pastors signed a covenant of unity. All-night prayer rallies began in earnest. More than 50,000 Christians attended these quarterly meetings. In some cases the facilities were provided free, with the condition that prayer be offered for the mayor and city leaders.

The atmosphere of the city began to change. Explosive church growth followed. Twenty-four-hour prayer was instituted. Mega churches emerged where fledgling fellowships had existed before. Many churches were forced to multiple services on Sunday.

> Our prayer for a spiritual awakening will without question be most effective if we take up the work of interceding for certain individuals in particular.[33]
> – O. Hallesby

> There is a hunger for God everywhere. You can see it on buses, on the streets and in the cafes. Anywhere you go people are ready to talk.[34]

Kiambu, Kenya

Kiambu, Kenya is a small city northwest of Nairobi. The little town was under the spiritual control of a local witch named Mama Jane. Relentless poverty kept people in constant need. Alcoholism kept them in bondage. Violence was common and streets were not safe after dark. A group of intercessors gathered to pray. What followed was a power-encounter with Mama Jane. Intercession won. The witch's power over the city was broken. Revival touched the whole community. Crime plummeted. Rape and murder ceased. The economy caught fresh wind. New buildings sprang up. The church that spearheaded the intercession grew to 5,000 members. The city previously had no church larger than 100 members. Now other churches are breaking through what had seemed a glass ceiling impeding congregational size.[35] Pastor Muthee says the whole city is grateful. They realize that the positive things happening in the city are traceable to the spiritual victories won by the prayers of the church.

Could It Happen Again?

Needed – A Fresh Vessel

Elisha asked the men of Jericho for a fresh, unused vessel and salt for the bitter water. A new and fresh vessel is so often what God uses to bring a Great Awakening! He looks to men and women. He is now looking for a fresh vessel - a Jonathan Edwards, a David Brainerd, a Luther, a William Seymour, a Richard Spurling – in this generation. Elisha asked to be taken to the source of the water in the city. Water is often a metaphor for the Spirit (Psalm 1:3; John 4:14; 7:37-39). Using the new vessel, he poured salt, a purifier, into the water. That is what God is looking for - a new vessel, an agent of cultural purity. The one common denominator to these great men is prayer. Leonard Ravenhill said "the blessed Holy Spirit could write the life of Elijah, Elisha's mentor in two words: 'He prayed.'" Time with God is the key to holiness and power, to impact and cultural transformation.

George Otis says that some 300 communities around the world have experienced some level of community transformation traceable to unified prayer efforts by humble leaders who long to see God manifest, not simply in their churches, but in their cities. Five characteristics are common.

1. Persevering leadership (Nehemiah 6:1-16);
2. Fervent, united prayer (Jonah 3:5-10);
3. Social Reconciliation (Matthew 5:23, 24; 18:15-20);
4. Public Power Encounters (Acts 9:32-35);
5. Diagnostic Research/Spiritual Mapping (Joshua 18:8-10).[36]

We see prayer from the perspective of our prayer closet or small prayer group. We hear our own weak and frail voice crying out for revival and renewal. It is as if the Evil One whispers, "It is all in vain. You are all alone." From heaven's perspective, the view is so different. From there you and I are not alone. It is as if "the whole of Christendom, all devout Christians," are standing together,[37] petitioning heaven for a Great Awakening. We are not alone when we pray. Our voices join the thousands of others, perhaps millions, praying at the same time. Heaven has to hear such pleas.

"God shapes the world by prayer!"[38] Our prayers live on after we die. They continue to influence events on the earth. God remembers us by such prayers. And he sets his heart on honoring the promise he made to us while we were on our knees. "That man is the most immortal who has done the most and best praying… The man of many and acceptable prayers has done the greatest service to the incoming generation. The prayers of God's saints strengthen the unborn generation against the desolating waves of sin and evil. Woe to the generations of sons whose fathers have been too busy to pray."[39]

Let's flood heaven with fresh pleas for a Great Awakening in America. Let's prayer walk every street in the nation. Let's rally intercessors to pray until a revival sweeps 30 million of the unsaved, unchurched population into the Kingdom of God. When revival comes, "a passion for repentance sweeps across specific geographic areas. Many people who had been unaware of the supernatural become keenly aware of it. They are stopped during their jobs as their minds are gripped by a terror of wrongdoing… throwing all else aside, they desperately search for a way of salvation."[40]

Ezekiel saw a river breaking forth from the temple. Flowing eastward, wherever the river went, it became a healing stream. The river, lined with fruitful trees, marched from Jerusalem to the Jordan valley and invaded the Dead Sea. When it did, Ezekiel said, that sea would live. Fishermen would line its banks and fish would fill their nets. What a vision! A river out of the house of God flowing to dead places causing them to live. A life giving force. Evangelists loading their boats with fresh disciples at places where no one had dared fish before!

Jesus seemed to reinforce this vision. In the midst of the water pouring ceremony in the Temple he cried out, *"If any man come to me, out of his belly shall flow rivers of living water!"* (John 7:38). The source of the river is not a place, but a person; not a building, but a people. You and I are the vessels that God is wanting to use to send forth a mighty stream of His Spirit that heals the land!

> I would rather stand against the raging cannons of the wicked than the fervent prayers of the righteous.
> - Unknown

The Evan Roberts Formula

Evan Roberts is viewed as the catalyst for the great Wales revival. So powerful was the impact of that awakening that crime dried up. Judges found themselves with empty courtrooms and policemen without calls. Bars closed. Illegitimacy birthrates plunged. Language changed. A cultural purging took place without new legal codes. Welshmen who worked the mines and used mules to bring the ore out found themselves radically changed by the revival. With gentler dispositions and purer speech, the mules could no longer understand them and had to be retained.

In six short months, 50,000 people were saved in Wales. Two million would be swept into the kingdom in England. The Wales revival was the driving force behind the Azusa Street awakening. What was the formula for such a mighty move of God. Evan Roberts called for four simple changes in the lives of cold Christians:

1. Repent of every known sin. Be brutally honest. Hide nothing.

2. Stop every doubtful habit. Even if it is not sin, if it is a hindrance in any way, cease to allow place for it in your life.

3. Go public with your witness. It is not permissible to be an anonymous Christian. Be humble, but be bold. Be gentle, but be forthright. Be public about your faith. Don't hide

your identity with Jesus or your love for him.

4. Follow the gentle promptings of the Holy Spirit. Dare to obey. Yield. Allow yourself to be an instrument. Trust your heart. Care not what others think, only seek the approval of God.

Here is the prayer Evan often prayed:

Father, I want to know you, but my cowardly heart fears to give up its toys. I cannot part with them without inward bleeding, and I do not try to hide from you the terror of the parting. I come trembling, but I do come. Please root from my heart all those things which I have cherished so long and which have become a very part of my living self, so that you may enter and dwell there without a rival. Then you shall make the place of your feet glorious. Then shall my heart have no need of the sun to shine in it, for You will be the light of it, and there shall be no night there.[41]

1. Bob Griffin, *Firestorms of Revival* (Lake Mary, FL: Strang Publications, 2006), 97.
2. *U.S. News and World Report*, "Cheating, Writing and Arithmetic: A New Epidemic of Fraud is Sweeping Through Our Schools," (November 22, 1999)
3. Griffin, 234.
4. Ibid, 6.
5. Geroge Barna, *The Index of Leading Spiritual Indicators*, 43.
6. Ibid, 51.
7. Ibid, 6.
8. Bill Bright, *The Coming Revival: America's Call to Fast, Pray, and 'Seek God's Face'* (Orlando. FL: W Life Publications, 1994), 19.
9. Griffin, 26.
10. Barna, 28-29.
11. David Barton, *Keys to Good Government* (WallBuilder Press: Aledo, TX; 1994), 18-19.
12. Ibid, 1.
13. Ibid, 17.
14. Ibid.
15. Chuck Colson, *Breakpoint*, December 30, 2004.
16. Barton,"America's Founding Fathers: Were they Christian?", 16
17. Samuel Chadwick, *The Path of Prayer* (CLC Publications, 2012), 89.
18. Alan Keyes, "The Corruption of America's Freedom," Bill Perkins, ed. *Steeling the Mind of America* (New Leaf Press: Green Forest, AR; 1997), 40.
19. Barna, 106.
20. George Barna, *The Second Coming of the Church* (Nashville, TN: Word, 1998), 6.
21. George Barna, *The Frog in the Kettle* (Ventura, CA: Regal, 1990), 138.
22. David Barton, *Keys to Good Government*, 2.
23. Henry Blackaby. *Holiness* (Nashville, TN: Broadman, 2003) 3.
24. Clyde Cranford, *Because We Love Him: Embracing a Life of Holiness* (Multnomah Publishing: Sisters, OR; 2002), 113.
25. Griffin, 210.
26. Brian H. Edwards, *Revival! A People Saturated With God* (Durham, England: Evangelical Press, 1990), 73-74.
27. Ibid, 73.
28. George Barna, "The Year's Most Intriguing Findings" (Barna Research Online, December 17, 2001, www.barna.org/FlexPage.aspx?Page=BarnaUpdate&BarnaUpdateID=84).
29. Griffin, 71.
30. Dutch Sheets, *Intercessory Prayer* (Ventura, CA: Regal, a division of Gospel Light, 1996), 23.
31. George Otis, Jr. *Informed Intercession* (Ventura, CA: Renew Books, a division of Gospel Light, 1999), 18.
32. Ibid, 18-23.
33. O. Hallesby. Prayer (Minneapolis, MN: Augsburg Publishing, 1931).

34 Ibid, 37-47.
35 Ibid, 48.
36 Otis, 56.
37 Martin Luther, "Luther's Way to Prayer," 74.
38 Bounds, *The Best of E. M. Bounds*, 75.
39 Ibid, 76.
40 James Burns, *The Laws of Revival* (Worldwide Publications: Wheaton, IL; 1993), 11.
41 A. W. Tozer, from the *Pursuit of God*. Quoted by Charles Swindoll, 94.

Final Note

On December 8, 1944, the phone rang in the office of the Third Army chaplain. On the other end was General George Patton. "How much praying is going on the Third Army?" The chaplain couldn't immediately provide an answer. The next question was more direct. "Do you have a good prayer for weather? We must do something about those rains if we are to win the war." The inclement weather had created a virtual stalemate. Outside, a steady rain fell. And Patton expected him to fix the problem? With prayer? The chaplain found no prayer for weather in his prayer books. He sat down and typed out a simple petition consisting of 70 words. He handed the prayer to Patton who read it and immediately ordered a quarter of a million copies printed and distributed to every soldier under his command.

The General seated himself, leaned back toying with a pencil,

Chaplain, I am a strong believer in prayer. There are three ways that men get what they want: by planning, by working, and by praying. Any great military operation takes careful planning or thinking. Then you must have well-trained troops to carry it out: that's working. But between the plan and the operation there is always an unknown. That unknown spells defeat or victory, success or failure. It is the reaction of the actors to the ordeal when it actually comes. Some people call that getting the breaks; I call it God. God has His part, or margin in everything. That's where prayer comes in. Up to now, in the Third Army, God has been very good to us. We have never retreated; we have suffered no defeats, no famine, no epidemics. This is because a lot of people back home are praying for us. We were lucky in Africa, in Sicily, and in Italy, simply because people prayed. But we have to pray for ourselves, too. A good soldier is not made merely by making him think and work. There is something in every soldier that goes deeper than thinking or working – it's his "guts." It is something that he has built in there: it is a world of truth and power that is higher than himself. Great living is not all output of thought and work. A man has to have intake as well. I don't know what you call it, but I call it religion, prayer, or God.[1]

If Patton was right, if prayer affects the circumstances that determine the outcome of wars, how can we win our present war, not against mortals, but against hell itself – without the whole army praying?

Watchman Nee believed,

Satan has in fact a plan against the saints of the Most High, which is to wear them out. Hence let us clearly recognize that the work of Satan in the lives of God's children is frequently not very noticeable, since his work is slowly to wear them down.

Let's not be 'worn down' or 'worn out' so that we cease to pray. We were saved to pray! Left on the earth to pray! We accomplish our greatest work by prayer. *"Continue in prayer,"* (Colossians 4:2). 'Whatever you do,' Paul would urge, *"don't stop praying."*

P. T. Forsyth charged,

The worst sin is prayerlessness. Overt sin, or crime, or the glaring inconsistencies which often surprise us in Christian people are the effect of this, or its punishment. We are left by God for lack of seeing Him. The history of the saints shows often that their lapses were the fruit and nemesis of slackness or neglect in prayer.

---

[1] The text of this article appeared in the October 6, 1971 issue of *The Review of the News*, which reprinted it from a 1950 government document. *The Review of the News* is a predecessor of THE NEW AMERICAN. See also: <www.thefreelibrary.com/The+true+story+of+the+Patton+Prayer%3a+the+author+of+General+Patton%27s+...-a0112356034>.

PRAYER
THE HEART OF IT ALL
Biblical Principles with Practical Models

RESOURCE KIT AVAILABLE

Includes:
- Book
- Personal Study Guide with Group It Section and Daily Devotions
- Flash Drive with Teaching Guide, PowerPoint file and video sessions

Use as a resource for personal growth or as a small group for discipleship study. Includes 14 sessions with support materials.

www.alivepublications.org

The Prayer Closet

Creating a Personal Prayer Room

Do you seek more than a disciplined, noble prayer routine, more than a daily prayer or the function of prayer and its benefits? Transform your relationship with God, one that is centered in the heart. Prayer is not something we do, it is someone we are with. And that needs a place! Includes prayer models, suggestions for your prayer room and discussion questions for personal review or group discussion.

BOOK AND RESOURCE KIT AVAILABLE

Use as a resource for personal growth or as a small group for discipleship study. Includes 12 sessions with support materials.

www.alivepublications.org

Host a
School of Prayer with P. Douglas Small

Schools of Prayer are seminars structured around learning and experiencing prayer.

Topics include:
- Enriching Your Personal Prayer Life
- Praying Through the Tabernacle
- Prayer the Heartbeat of the Church
- Heaven is a Courtroom
- Theology and Philosophy for Prayer Ministry
- Organizing Intercessors
- Entertaining God
- The Critical Strategic Uncomfortable Middle

www.projectpray.org
1-855-84-ALIVE

Pray for a Cause!
Banners for your church or event.

- Use as prayer points during a prayer assembly
- Promote prayer during certain times of the year, such as US Government during election time
- Place in your Prayer Center
- And many more uses!

Banners are available in 3 different sizes:

- Large 30×72 with stand.
- Small 30×48 with stand.
- Petite 18×36 with pole pocket to insert a dowel rod with rope for hanging (dowel and rope not included).

The Project Pray or Church of God logo can be printed at the bottom of the banner for free. Or print your church's logo for an extra $10 for the first banner and $5 for each additional banner.

View all banner themes and order online at:
www.alivepublications.org